MAKE

THE

TEAM

PQI429840

THE ART OF SELF-RECRUITING

The Step-by-Step Guide to making the college soccer team that's right for you

AVI STOPPER

MAKE THE TEAM

THE ART OF SELF-RECRUITING

AVI STOPPER

International Standard Book Number: 0-615-12611-1

Library of Congress Catalog Card Number: 2004109646

This book is designed to provide accurate and authoritative
information with respect to the subject matter covered. It is sold
with the understanding that the author and publisher is not en-
gaged in rendering legal, accounting, or other professional services. If legal advice or other expert assistance is required, the
services of a competent attorney or professional person should
be sought. While every attempt is made to provide accurate information, the author and publisher cannot be held accountable
for any errors or omissions.

Printed in the United States of America.

This book, quite simply, would never have gotten this far were it not for the unwavering support of Kapi Monoyios, whose extraordinary creativity, enthusiasm, and vision are manifest on every page.

TO THE READER

Playing college soccer is a wonderful experience. It will enrich your time in college and leave you with life-long friends and memories.

This book is intended to **clarify the recruiting process and help you maximize your chances of winning a spot on the college team that's right for you.** Getting your hands on *Make the Team* is a big step towards a successful college soccer career.

As a college soccer coach, I conceived *self-recruiting* during a particularly frustrating series of recruiting experiences. I realized that many high school players just don't know how to effectively communicate with college coaches. Instead of marketing themselves they wait and hope to be contacted.

I reflected on my own experience as a recruit, which was similarly hamstrung by inexperience with the process. I didn't know how to communicate with coaches. Nor did I know how to get seen by the right coaches and convince them that I was right for their teams.

What it came down to was luck. I was fortunate enough to stumble backwards into a wonderful college soccer experience. Many other players were not so lucky.

As a college coach now, I know that there are countless qualified players out there who never get out of the recruiting starting blocks. Of those who do make progress, many wander off in the wrong direction. *Make the Team* is a response to these problems.

Self-recruiting is demanding. If you're committed to having a successful college soccer career, you must take the initiative to make it happen. By dedicating yourself to self-recruiting, you will dramatically improve your chances of making the team. So get to it!

CONTENTS

PART V: ON-FIELD SELF-RECRUITING

PART VI: DELIBERATION, NEGOTIATION & MAKING A DECISION

PART VII: THE FINAL PUSH

APPENDICES

INTRODUCTION

When you're out on the soccer field, you can stand around and wait, hoping that the ball will eventually come to you. Or, you can be active, mentally involved, and constantly working to make things happen.

The same is true with college soccer recruiting. You can sit around waiting for college coaches to discover you. Maybe they will, maybe they won't. If they do discover you, their schools might end up being completely wrong for you.

By contrast, **you can take control of college recruiting**. You can be active and involved. You can market yourself to the schools that *you* like, to ensure that you end up in a college soccer environment that's right for you.

Being assertive and taking control of the process is the best way to ensure a successful outcome. That's what this book is all about: **self-recruiting**.

Self-Recruiting is the process **for boys and girls** where *you* determine the colleges that interest you, *you* choose the coaches you want to play for, and *you* demonstrate that you are qualified for their teams.

THE SELF-RECRUITING METHOD an overview of the process...

PREPARATION

- Determine the type of academic, social, and athletic college **environment** that's right for you.

- Identify **candidate schools** where such an environment exists—pick colleges that feel right for you.

- Assess the colleges and soccer programs—if any—that have **contacted you**.

- **Organize** yourself. Make a file folder for each college to keep all e-mails, letters, notes on phone coversations, etc. in a central location.

CORRESPONDENCE

- Write a **cover letter and resume**, introducing yourself and your accomplishments. Sell yourself on paper.

- **Follow-up** on your cover letter and resume.

- Send a **schedule** of your games and tournaments.

- Provide **regular updates** and progress reports—maintain monthly contact with each coach.

- Make a highlights **video**.

APPEARANCES

- Attend college soccer **camps**.

- Arrange for coaches to see you at **tournaments**.

- **Visit** colleges. See the campuses of the schools that interest you most.

DECISION-MAKING

- Decide which schools you're going to apply to. **Apply**.

- **Inform** coaches that you've applied to their schools.

- **Notify** coaches when you've been accepted.

- Weigh your **options**. Compare and contrast the qualities of each school and soccer program—including any **scholarship** offers.

- Make a **commitment**—in certain cases, make a *verbal commitment* or sign a *letter of intent*.

SUMMER PREPARATIONS

- **Update** the coach regularly throughout the summer before your freshman season.

- Get **fit**.

- Maximize your chances to **walk-on** if the coach has not offered you a recruited spot on the team.

ICON KEY

 **LETTERS** - Hard-copy correspondence that you should mail to coaches: letters, resume, game schedules, etc.

 **PHONE CALLS** - Calls that you should make to coaches, and pointers on what to say.

 PARENTS - Ways in which parents can be especially helpful during the self-recruiting process.

 **FILE FOLDERS** - Letters, brochures, notes, etc. that should be stored in your organized file system.

 E-MAIL - Notes, updates, schedules, and reminders you should send coaches via e-mail.

 FREQUENTLY ASKED QUESTION - Important questions about which high school players and their parents are often misinformed.

 IMPORTANT ASIDE - Points that will enhance your understanding and overall effectiveness with self-recruiting.

 OUT OF THE RECRUITING SPOTLIGHT - Pointers for recruits who college coaches haven't yet discovered.

 NEAR THE RECRUITING SPOTLIGHT - Pointers for recruits who have received some attention from college coaches.

 IN THE RECRUITING SPOTLIGHT - Pointers for recruits who are getting a lot of personal attention from college coaches.

 WARNING! - Pitfalls that can derail or sidetrack your self-recruiting efforts. Heed all warning signs!

PART I

GETTING STARTED

If you've made it this far into the book, you probably have more than a fleeting interest in playing soccer in college.

What you hold in your hands is a guide that will lead you through the murky waters of college recruiting.

By following this strategy you will increase your chances of playing soccer in college.

1

SELF-RECRUITING: MARKETING YOURSELF

The theme of this book is self-promotion, not as bragging or being egotistical, but in terms of marketing yourself to college coaches. In other words, if you are committed to playing soccer in college, **you have to make it happen**. Don't just hope that some coach will see you and decide that you're his or her next superstar.

DO IT YOURSELF

The reality is that only a tiny fraction of high school soccer players are actively recruited by coaches. Other players have to go out and do the recruiting themselves, or else risk not playing in college.

> *Do I have to be the best player on my club and/or high school team to play college soccer?*
>
> No. As long as you're a relatively good player there's probably a college team out there that needs you.
>
> You don't have to be an ODP standout, or an All-State selection for that matter. However, your resume should probably include a few years as a starter for your high school team and a strong club soccer background. College coaches are generally not looking for recreational players.

There are good college soccer opportunities for just about every reasonably good high school soccer player. You don't have to be the best player on your team to play college soccer. Drive, motivation, and the desire to succeed count for a lot. More than anything, **you should not be ashamed about wanting to play college soccer**. It's an admirable goal.

There are, of course, college soccer opportunities for kids who are tremendous players as well as great students. Yet there are also great situations for excellent students who are aren't the best players. There are also teams for strong players who aren't in the top tier academically.

HUNDREDS OF COLLEGE TEAMS

Most people are aware of only a few high-profile college soccer teams.

There are actually more than 2,000 teams out there.

	# of Women's Teams	# of Men's Teams
NCAA Division I	280	200
NCAA Division II	200	170
NCAA Division III	390	370
NAIA	220	230

The first key component of self-recruiting *(discussed in detail in Chapters 5 & 6)* is to accurately **identify a handful of colleges that meet your academic and social needs**. Then investigate the soccer programs of those candidate schools with the same rigor that you evaluated the rest of the school.

Consult sources like college profile books, college counselors, and the internet to identify the schools that seem right for you academically, socially, and athletically.

Once you've identified the right schools for you, this book will help you make a strong self-recruiting pitch and improve your chances of making the team.

Recruiting services are companies you pay to match you with a college soccer program. They notoriously overcharge and underachieve.

Recruiting services exploit people's insecurities, trumpeting their expertise and your inexperience. Yet across the country, college coaches' recycling bins are brimming with recruiting service solicitations for unqualified students. Put simply: you're wasting your money if a recruiting service is touting you and your 980 SATs to a college with a 1310 average.

What it boils down to is that you need to dedicate yourself to researching schools that are appropriate academically, socially, and athletically. You don't want someone who doesn't even know you determining where you should go to college.

College literature is broadly available on the internet and in bookstores. Take the Sunday afternoon research excursion to your local bookstore *(described in Chapter 6.)* In those few hours you will accomplish a hundred times—at a hundredth of the cost—what a recruiting service can offer you.

LAYOUT OF THE BOOK

The organization of the chapters in this book outlines the ideal timing and *order of operations*. Self-recruiting and the college application process, however, vary from person to person. So feel free to skim chapters and skip around.

Your **cover letter and resume** *(Chapters 8-9)* **are one exception to the flexibility of self-recruiting**. Your cover letter and resume should always be your first formal communication with a coach.

Before plowing ahead, **first skim through the book to get an overview of the process**. From the outset, you should familiarize yourself with certain aspects of the process—especially Chapter 22, on academic eligibility and the NCAA Clearinghouse. You might also want to look over the chapters on scholarships and campus visits.

SELF-RELIANCE

To be successful with recruiting, you must take personal responsibility for the process. **Getting recognized by a coach is up to you.**

Though the task of self-recruiting ultimately falls to you, the player, college selection can be a lot to chew on. **So work through this book with your parents**.

SELF-RECRUITING ON & OFF THE FIELD

A dynamic, multidimensional marketing pitch will make you a strong candidate. To that end, self-recruiting involves *on-field* and *off-field* components.

On-field self-recruiting refers to real-life appearances in which a coach can evaluate your play. **Off-field self-recruiting**, though perhaps less obvious, **is no less critical**. It is the all-important exchange of information, the dialogue in which you engage a coach. Demonstrate to coaches that you are enthusiastic, responsible, and dedicated.

On-field and off-field self-recruiting are equally important. They are both critical to self-recruiting success.

PARENTS

Selecting a college is a daunting task for most high school students. The sheer number of colleges is enough to make even the most self-possessed 17 year-old quake at least a little. Ultimately, the student must be motivated to drive the college selection and self-recruiting process forward. But **THERE ARE NUMEROUS TIMES WHEN A PARENT'S GUIDANCE AND ASSISTANCE ARE INVALUABLE.**

As parents, concentrate on what is right for your child. If he's not Harvard material, don't push him in that direction. Don't be overbearing and run the show yourself. College coaches are recruiting players, not players' parents. In sum, help your child work through this book. Throughout the process, you can provide invaluable support and direction.

GUIDE, DON'T DOMINATE

- Help your child identify ten or so legitimate candidate schools.

- Encourage him to turn off the television, sit down, and write a cover letter and resume. Help edit, but don't censor.

- Assist with keeping self-recruiting materials organized.

- Make sure he's being diligent about maintaining regular contact with the coaches at his candidate schools.

- Address the financial issues—a complicated and touchy component of the college selection process that will stump most young people.

- When he child reaches an impasse, help him work through it.

- When the situation demands that you speak with a college coach, do so.

2

THE GOAL OF SELF-RECRUITING

Though the goal of self-recruiting may seem simple, many prospective college athletes have only a basic understanding of recruiting, and aren't clear as to what they're actually trying to accomplish.

Generally speaking, it's straightforward: you contact a college coach because you want to play soccer for his team. But beyond that, let's be more specific about what exactly you're trying to achieve.

RECRUIT vs. WALK-ON

The terms "recruit" and "walk-on" underscore an important distinction in recruiting and college athletics. It's the difference between being assured a spot on a college team, and being uncertain as to whether you'll make the team. As a prospective student athlete, **you want to be a recruit and not have to walk-on**.

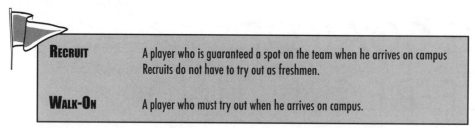

| **RECRUIT** | A player who is guaranteed a spot on the team when he arrives on campus Recruits do not have to try out as freshmen. |
| **WALK-ON** | A player who must try out when he arrives on campus. |

College coaches place a premium on the few precious weeks of pre-season they have to prepare their teams. Most coaches want to spend these practices working closely with the players that they know will be on the team. **Freshman recruits are invited to pre-season practices**. There are no tryouts for recruits.

Most coaches conduct open tryouts during the first pre-season week, in the morning or afternoon when they are not working with their core group of players. Recruits do not participate in tryouts. **For walk-ons, however, tryouts represent the proving grounds**; tryouts are a make-it-or-break-it situation for walk-ons.

The Ideal Outcome

The best outcome of self-recruiting is to be a recruit, to be promised a position on the team well before you arrive on campus. You don't have to try out; **as a recruited player, you are a guaranteed member of the team**.

A Contingency Plan

Say you've decided to attend a particular school and desperately want to be on the soccer team. Though you've self-recruited vigorously, the coach hasn't offered you a recruited position. Instead she's suggested that you come to walk-on tryouts.

Such a situation is not ideal, but also not hopeless. You must **continue to self-recruit so the coach knows you well by the time you arrive on campus**. The coach's familiarity with you will help distinguish you from the pack during tryouts.

A sign posted once at Princeton varsity athletic tryouts read, *"If we don't know you, don't come out."*

The message is loud and clear: **MAKE YOURSELF WELL-KNOWN TO COLLEGE COACHES BEFORE YOU ARRIVE ON CAMPUS.**

WHERE TO BEGIN

- **Don't expect coaches to come banging down your door**. If they do, great. Yet there are numerous factors that limit the scope of college coaches' recruiting—money, time, geography, and a dizzying number of potential players.

  Faced with college coaches' recruiting limitations, it's up to you to be assertive and get your name out there.

- **Have some conversations with your current coaches** about what they think is the right college *level* for you. You don't have to ask them to suggest specific schools—that's not their area of expertise.

- Talk to players you know who have gone on to play college soccer. What do they think is right for you?

- Start thinking about **what you really want out of your overall college experience**.

- **Enlist your parents' help** in working through this book.

- Dedicate yourself to finding and securing the *right* environment. An investment of your time and energy now will pay off down the road.

Make Yourself A Stronger Candidate

In the end, your play will have to do a lot of the talking.

Self-recruiting will not make you a better player. It will, however, help you become a stronger candidate for the schools and soccer programs that fit your academic and athletic qualifications.

Even as you self-recruit, you should be working to improve yourself as a player.

In tandem, self-recruiting and a lot of practice are a potent combination— one that will make you a stronger candidate overall.

PEOPLE WHO CAN HELP

If you're serious about playing college soccer you have to take the lead role in making it happen. Commit yourself to it; don't expect others to do it for you.

Though the interest and determination must originate from you, THERE ARE MANY PEOPLE ALONG THE WAY WHO CAN HELP, including:

- **PARENTS**
- **SIBLINGS & RELATIVES**
- **TEACHERS**
- **COUNSELORS**
- **CLUB COACHES**
- **HIGH SCHOOL COACHES**
- **CURRENT COLLEGE PLAYERS**
- **FORMER COLLEGE PLAYERS**

BE DIGNIFIED

You should always keep in mind that recruiting is not an exercise in supplication. Don't throw yourself at a coach's feet and beg for a spot on the team. In a calm, collected, and confident fashion, demonstrate to the coach that you are qualified for his team.

A qualified recruit who initiates and maintains contact is a coach's dream come true. If you present yourself in an organized, compelling fashion, you will have saved a coach time and money. Your efforts will be rewarded. So get on with it.

3

THE RECRUITING SPOTLIGHT

By the time you start thinking seriously about college soccer—not just in an abstract, *"Yeah, I think I'd like to play soccer in college,"* sense—you might already have received solicitations from a coach or two. For that matter, you may have received a mountain of mail from one coach who is intent on winning your services. By contrast, you might still be anonymous, an unidentified treasure eager to reveal yourself to the college soccer world.

When you start self-recruiting, you'll find yourself in one of these categories:

OUT OF THE SPOTLIGHT

Unidentified Recruits—A coach doesn't know you. You're not in the spotlight—yet! Committed self-recruiting will put you exactly where you want to be.

NEAR THE SPOTLIGHT

Recruits of Interest—A coach has seen you play, and is generally interested. He wants to find out more about you. The spotlight is moving in your direction.

IN THE SPOTLIGHT

Priority Recruits—A coach is heavily invested in recruiting you. He's written you a few personal letters and made repeated overtures. The recruiting spotlight is trained directly on you.

Relax if you're not yet in the spotlight. Your clear objective is to gain priority status. **Committed self-recruiting will thrust you into a prominent position**.

For top recruits, self-recruiting is no less important than for players in the other categories. Don't squander your status through apathy and inaction. If you are interested in a school that recruits you heavily, work to develop a strong relationship with the coach. Be responsive and enthusiastic. Self-recruiting will secure your standing.

The bottom line is that self-recruiting is applicable for players in each category. Though the details of each player's recruiting experience vary, the theme is universal: whatever your initial status, self-recruiting will propel you onto a college team.

FAQ

My teammates have received recruiting solicitations but I have not. If I am not "in the spotlight" does it mean that college coaches have determined that I am not capable of playing college soccer?

No. Don't be deterred by coaches' oversight. Imagine the vast pool of high school players a college soccer coach has to sift through. **IF YOU HAVEN'T BEEN "IDENTIFIED" DON'T RESIGN YOURSELF TO NOT PLAYING COLLEGE SOCCER.** Instead you must commit yourself to going out and making it happen.

If your teammates are being recruited, it may actually be for schools that aren't right for them academically and/or socially.

Additionally, many coaches send out bulk mailings, which are little more than a shot in the dark. To counter this inefficiency, you must personalize the recruiting process and make it more targeted. You determine which schools are right for you and then you work for the attention of those coaches.

4

TIMING

The recruiting timeline is a subject of great confusion. Jittery players hear whispers in the grass, rumors that spread like wildfire.

The rumor mill spawns myths like, *"If it's the spring of your junior year and you haven't been contacted by any coaches, you have no chance of playing soccer in college."* That's just wrong.

Instead, hearsay is usually way off the mark. If you are a second-semester junior, you should definitely get moving. Yet even if you are a first-semester senior there's still time to make an effective self-recruiting pitch. **College coaches may not be as far ahead with recruiting as you think.**

In reality, **most coaches don't finalize their recruiting classes until the winter or spring of the recruits' senior year in high school**. A coach has to wait for a recruit to apply. Then the coach must wait to see if the recruit is accepted. Once acceptance letters are mailed, the coach has to convince the recruit to enroll.

From the coach's end, recruiting is a long, tiring process. With self-recruiting, you will make it easier for him! It's a mutually beneficial arrangement.

> **YOU CAN BEGIN SELF-RECRUITING AT ANY POINT IN YOUR HIGH SCHOOL CAREER.** Even if it's late in the spring of your senior year, and you know where you're going in the fall but haven't finalized your standing with the college team, following this strategy will maximize your chances of getting on the team.
>
> This is by no means an endorsement of procrastination. Start the process early. Self-recruiting is most effective when you don't have to rush.

THE BEST TIME TO START

For most players, **the best time to start self-recruiting is during the fall or winter of your junior year.**

Consider waiting until your fall season has ended before you initiate contact with college coaches. From this point on you must have *regular contact* with the coaches until you decide which college you will attend.

By waiting until your junior fall season is over, you can include your most recent statistics, photographs, and accolades in your soccer cover letter and resume.

Also, winter weather and limited daylight aren't great conditions for playing soccer. The winter months, however, are perfect for an indoors project like self-recruiting. **You can devote the time you normally spend at practice to getting yourself onto a college soccer team**. Believe me, it's a worthwhile trade.

During the winter, college coaches spend a lot of time in their offices. For an active breed, this is almost insufferable. Coaches gaze out the window daydreaming, wishing the snow would melt.

Most coaches concentrate on recruiting during the long winter months to pass the time productively.

EARLY STARTS

There will always be those players who start writing coaches while still in the tender clutches of their freshman and sophomore years. If this is your style, go for it.

To effectively self-recruit, though, **you have to maintain regular contact with coaches for the duration of your time in high school**. If as an enterprising sophomore you write a coach and then proceed to fall off the face of the earth until your senior year, you haven't done yourself any good.

If you do start self-recruiting as a sophomore, in addition to maintaining regular contact with your candidate coaches, you should send an updated resume after your junior fall season.

The bottom line for would-be early starters: **Begin self-recruiting only when you're prepared to invest yourself consistently**. You *must* correspond with your candidate coaches regularly—not just sporadically, when the spirit moves you.

Early Starts For Premier Players

The recruiting timeline is accelerated for high school players who are considered the top prospects in the country—those who have extensive regional and national team experience, or are central players on high profile club teams.

Many top players will be heavily courted by college coaches. If this is the case for you, **don't make the coach do all the work**. Active self-recruiting will solidify your candidacy. **Show the coach—who's clearly enthusiastic about you—that you're just as excited about playing for him**.

Elite Girls: Start Spring of Sophomore Year

In recent years, the top handful of Division I women's programs in the country have accelerated recruiting by a year. Recruiting is sometimes finished as early as the fall of a recruiting class's junior year in high school—which is to say that by the spring, coaches of some elite women's teams **are looking almost exclusively at sophomores**.

Admissions departments do an *"early read"* of a recruit's credentials and report to the coach whether the player will likely be accepted. If all parties agree that it's a good fit, the coach will request a *verbal commitment* from the player. *(See Chapter 24.)*

ELITE BOYS: START SUMMER BEFORE JUNIOR YEAR

The timeline is also accelerated for elite college men's teams—though not to the extent of women's recruiting. One possible explanation is that boys physically develop later in high school. A sophomore boy who's the biggest, baddest player on his team will not necessarily be the big dog in two years.

No less, the top few Division I men's programs solidify their recruiting classes relatively early—**often during the late fall of a player's senior year of high school**.

LATE STARTS

All is not lost for those—including the author—who decide to pursue college soccer midway through their senior year of high school. Some opportunities may have already passed, but there still is hope. You must move quickly yet carefully to select your candidate schools and correspond with the coaches.

TIMELINE VARIABLES

The self-recruiting timeline varies from person to person and depends on a number of factors including:

TIMEFRAME
The point in your high school career when you begin self-recruiting. If you're a sophomore beginning the process, self-recruiting will occur over a longer timeframe than that of a senior who's just beginning.

QUALIFICATIONS
The athlete's appearance on paper. If you have national team experience, a coach will probably make a swift effort to see you play.

ACCESSIBILITY
How close you live or play to a given school. The closer you are, the easier it is for a coach to see you play.

MARKETING
How effectively you market yourself will determine your success in the recruitment process.

> Self-recruiting is applicable whether you start late, early, or right on time. Be persistent if the initial response isn't dazzling.
>
> Your efforts should always be aimed at reaching an agreement with a coach that you will enter the team as a recruit.
>
> If it comes to walk-on tryouts, don't lose heart, and don't stop self-recruiting. Follow the steps outlined in Chapter 25 to maximize your chances.

SUGGESTED TIMELINES

One of the questions that's asked most frequently is: **"WHAT SHOULD I BE DOING RIGHT NOW TO GET MYSELF ON A COLLEGE TEAM?"**

In an effort to answer that type of question, Appendix A (at the back of the book) provides a wide range of suggested self-recruiting timelines. These timelines list the self-recruiting steps that you should be taking at a given time in your high school career, based on when you begin the process.

If, for example, you started self-recruiting during the fall of your junior year and you're trying to figure out what to do that winter and spring, consult the timeline that's titled **"IF YOU START DURING YOUR...JUNIOR YEAR—LATE FALL."** The timeline looks like this:

J U N I O R	W I N T E R	Send your spring schedule. Determine which summer camps the coach will attend. Register for camp.
	S P R I N G	Keep the coach posted on your season. Arrange for the coach to see you play in a tournament. Follow up on-field appearances with correspondence.

Hence, during the winter of your junior year you should focus on sending coaches your spring schedule, determining which summer camps the coaches will attend, and registering for one of those camps.

That spring, you want to keep the coach updated on your season, try to arrange for him to see you play in person, and then follow up those on-field appearances with a phone call or e-mail.

The timelines list the highlights of self-recruiting. In addition to the steps listed, **YOU MUST MAINTAIN REGULAR CONTACT WITH YOUR CANDIDATE COACHES AT ALL TIMES.**

PART II

PREPARATION

As you embark on your self-recruiting adventure you must **be honest with yourself about your ability**.

Choose candidate schools and teams that are within your academic and athletic range.

In soccer and other aspects of your life, think about what it is that you really want out of your college experience.

5

THE RIGHT FIT

The first task of self-recruiting is a candid self-evaluation. On your own and with your parents, you must determine the academic and athletic environment that is right for you. How good of a student are you? How good of a player are you? These are the questions you have to ask yourself to figure out what kind of school will be right for you.

ACADEMICS AS THE PRIORITY

In determining the right type of school, you have to take academics into account first and foremost. Do not sacrifice your intellectual potential just to play soccer in college.

The odds of playing professional soccer after college are slim. It's far more likely that **after college you'll have to take your academic and intellectual credentials out into the world and get a job**.

That said, you might be someone who values soccer so much that you are only willing to go to a school where you'll be able to play. It may mean compromising your Ivy League academic qualifications to play soccer at the University of Jupiter's Twelfth Moon.

The good news is that **colleges are so numerous and diverse that if you look hard enough you can find the right mix of athletics and academics**.

For example, if you're qualified for schools within a certain academic tier, but aren't the greatest player, you might have to consider the weaker teams within that tier. If this is the case, you should research conferences comprised of schools with strong academics but less-strong athletics.

BE HONEST ABOUT YOUR ABILITY

Be practical. **Don't just go for the most glamorous soccer names**. If you're really stretching—i.e. you're clearly unqualified for a team—**even if you make the team, you may find yourself on the bench for four dismal years**.

Challenge yourself athletically, but be realistic and find a place where you know you'll play. If you're not qualified to play at Indiana, North Carolina, Notre Dame, or UCLA, don't waste your time—or theirs. If, however, you are truly a player of that caliber, by all means go for it.

Take advantage of the resources at your disposal. **Speak frankly with your high school and club coaches about what they think is an appropriate college soccer environment for you**. Talk to other people who are connected to college sports and have seen you play. Guidance counselors can offer insight as can recent graduates from your school who play in college.

DIVISION I? II? III? NAIA?

The issue of college divisions is a source of great confusion. People often talk about Division I in adoring terms. There is much well-deserved prestige associated with playing for a top-tier Division I school. Yet there are actually a number of DII and DIII teams out there that can compete with some DI teams. Just because a school is DI doesn't mean that its soccer team is top caliber.

It's great if your self-assessment and college search lead to Division I schools. But it's no less of a success if you determine that the overall environment in DII, DIII, or the NAIA is better for you. This process is about **finding the right place** for you, which **is not always going to be the most glitzy**.

COLLEGIATE DIVISIONS

NCAA DIVISION I	Generally larger schools; athletic scholarships are allowed—except in the Ivy League; year-round commitment with abbreviated winter and spring seasons; national travel; elite competition among the top teams; concentration on top teams of the best players in the country.
NCAA DIVISION II	Athletic scholarships are allowed, though fewer than DI; some competition against DI schools; year-round commitment; limited national travel—generally more regional; very strong players, many international.
NCAA DIVISION III	No athletic scholarships; many academically elite small colleges; intense regional competition; limited non-traditional seasons; many excellent players.
NAIA	Generally small schools; recruiting guidelines that are less restrictive than those of the NCAA; athletic scholarships are allowed; compete mostly with other NAIA schools; regional competition; can transfer without sitting out a season.

ATHLETICS & YOUR SOCIAL LIFE

Anyone who has played college soccer will tell you that **it's a major commitment**. In addition to games, daily practices, and tape viewings, you'll have team meals, meetings, and travel. It's no small investment of time and energy.

Some teams take extended trips across the country that force players to miss classes. Some schools find ways to accommodate athletes who miss scheduled tests, etc. Others tolerate absence grudgingly and make you jump through hoops to reschedule tests and assignments.

Many soccer teams also have time-consuming winter and spring seasons, which further complicate an athlete's pursuit of other interests.

By comparison, other teams practice informally during the off-season, allowing students to sample some of the abundant opportunities in college, including music, theater, dance, and student government.

In college there are endless opportunities beyond soccer to pursue. **Committing to a soccer team means sacrificing some of those opportunities**. Ask yourself if you're willing to make that sacrifice.

DETERMINING THE RIGHT FIT

Think long and hard about the overall experience you want out of college. Tap into any resources you can find. Talk with your parents, teachers, coaches, and college counselors. **Accurately identifying a pool of candidate schools will put you well on your way to success.**

Though it may be intimidating initially, the diversity among colleges actually works in your favor. **It's highly likely that there is some place out there that will be a great fit for you**.

First, determine what kind of school is right for you. After that, a good way to proceed is to investigate specific conferences or schools you've heard about. If you know of a college through hearsay or because your neighbor's cousin goes there and loves it, check it out.

QUESTIONS TO DETERMINE THE RIGHT FIT

- What kind of school are you QUALIFIED FOR ACADEMICALLY?

- What level college soccer team are you QUALIFIED FOR AS A PLAYER? Get input from your club and high school coaches and other knowledgeable acquaintances.

- What BALANCE OF ACADEMICS, SOCIAL LIFE, ATHLETICS, AND OTHER EXTRACURRICULAR ACTIVITIES do you want?

- Are you willing to COMMIT A SUBSTANTIAL AMOUNT OF YOUR TIME in college to varsity soccer?

- What FINANCIAL ARRANGEMENTS will you need for schools within various tuition brackets? Can you afford tuition, or will you qualify for need-based financial aid or an academic or athletic scholarship? Are you willing to take out a loan to finance your education?

- What GEOGRAPHICAL REGION of the country do you prefer? Do you want to be near your parents, so they can come see your games?

- What SIZE school is right for you? Do you prefer the dynamism of a large campus environment, or the intimacy of a small campus?

Outline What You're Looking For

Take a pencil and a piece of paper and answer the preceding questions. This will help you organize your thoughts as to what you want your college experience to be like.

MOOKIE'S COLLEGE CONSIDERATIONS

Willingness to Commit to Soccer:

I'm very enthusiastic about playing soccer in college.

Academic Credentials:

Strong, but not the best. 1100 SAT/3.1 GPA.

Athletic Ability:

I'm one of the better players on a relatively strong team.

Extracurricular Activities:

I want to have time to pursue other things outside of soccer, especially surfing.

Financial Considerations:

I will not qualify for need-based aid. I need low tuition or a scholarship of some sort.

Location:

California coast.

School Size:

Small to medium.

MOOKIE WOULD THEN REVIEW HIS NOTES AND SAY:

"Okay, so what I'm looking for is a medium-sized school in California where I can play soccer at a moderately competitive level and also surf on a regular basis. I'm solid academically and athletically, but probably not tops in either category. I'm not going to qualify for need-based financial aid, so I need a situation in which tuition is not exorbitant or where I can get an athletic or academic scholarship."

NOW MOOKIE NEEDS TO GO DO SOME RESEARCH TO IDENTIFY CANDIDATE SCHOOLS THAT SATISFY THESE REQUIREMENTS.

 **PARENTS**

Choosing a college can be intimidating for even the most self-aware high school students. Help guide your child through the murky waters to a more clear understanding of what it is that he wants out of his college experience.

Sit down and discuss these issues with your son or daughter to help determine what type of college you should be looking for.

6

IDENTIFYING CANDIDATE SCHOOLS

Having completed the exercise in the previous chapter, you should have a better idea of the academic, social, and athletic environment that's right for you. Now you need to generate a pool of ten or so candidate schools that fit your profile.

To be successful with self-recruiting, **you have to carefully hand-select colleges that are right for you**.

FIND THE RIGHT SCHOOLS

Accurately identifying candidate schools is a huge step forward. If you self-recruit to schools that aren't right for you, the outcome might not be so favorable. To turn the odds in your favor you should spend considerable time researching colleges.

As you evaluate candidate schools ask yourself this essential question: **"Would I still want to go here if I couldn't play soccer?"** If the answer is no, you should look elsewhere.

TAKE CONTROL OF THE PROCESS

Don't just get sucked into following the one or two random leads that find their way to your mailbox. If you have only been contacted by the coaches at Desolate Atoll University and Middle of Nowhere College, **you do not have to limit your college search to those schools**.

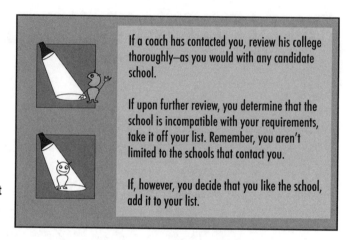

If a coach has contacted you, review his college thoroughly—as you would with any candidate school.

If upon further review, you determine that the school is incompatible with your requirements, take it off your list. Remember, you aren't limited to the schools that contact you.

If, however, you decide that you like the school, add it to your list.

Why should a couple of coaches who happened to notice you dictate your future? You have the right to decide which schools are best for you. Of course a school that contacts you may turn out to be the perfect fit, so you shouldn't rule it out automatically.

 **PARENTS**

Identifying the right colleges is a critical stage in self-recruiting. It's also one in which YOUR ASSISTANCE CAN MAKE A MAJOR DIFFERENCE. Here's how you can help. Odds are that you know a lot about your kid, and more about specific colleges than he or she knows.

Based on the conversations you had in Chapter 5 to determine the right fit, HELP YOUR CHILD FIND CANDIDATE SCHOOLS THAT FIT THE BILL.

A great way to accomplish this is to do some research on your own and present your child with a list of thirty or so schools—pared down from the 3000 that are out there—that you think he should investigate.

RESEARCH CANDIDATE SCHOOLS

Researching colleges is a time-consuming, but worthwhile process. Talk to counselors, flip through college profile books, search the internet, and so on.

The more you learn about an assortment of colleges, the more discerning your selection of candidate schools, and the more likely you will be to succeed.

College Counselors

A handful of high schools employ full-time college counselors. Other schools rely on general guidance counselors to provide this service.

Find out what sort of college guidance is available at your school. Schedule a time to meet with the counselor. **Be prepared for your meeting with an idea of what you're looking for in a college**.

If the guidance counselor provides useful advice, continue to consult with him as you develop your pool of candidate schools. If your meeting with the college counselor doesn't work out so well, don't throw up your arms in despair.

Even if the college guidance at your school is excellent, it is unlikely that an accurate list of candidate schools will simply fall into your lap. Fortunately, there are vast print and internet resources out there for you to utilize.

College Profile Books

There are a number of major companies who make it their business to accurately portray colleges for college-bound high school students.

Books abound that profile the "Best 350 Colleges," "100 Great Schools at Great Prices," and so on. In these books, one or two pages are devoted to each college. The profiles, though brief, are enough to give you the gist of a school. Disregard those that sound terrible and dog-ear those that catch your eye.

College profile books are a fantastic place to start your search. If you spend a few hours flipping through one of these books you'll undoubtedly find a number of schools that pique your interest. And there, just like that, you'll have made progress.

> There are a few profile books out there that are based on college athletics alone.
>
> These books miss the fundamental point: college is most importantly an academic and social experience.
>
> You should select a college for its overall merits, not just because a book says that the school has a good soccer team.

The Internet

Type "college search" into any internet search engine, and you will find endless resources to help you identify candidate schools.

There are, of course, thousands of individual college websites. You should surf schools' websites once you've really begun to narrow down the field—otherwise you'll be at it forever.

There are also sites that briefly profile a number of colleges—the electronic version of the aforementioned profile books.

A number of excellent websites ask you a bunch of questions and then produce a list of schools that meet your criteria. Utilize any tool like this that helps you narrow the field.

TWO GOOD WAYS TO GET STARTED

Describing individual schools is beyond the scope of this book. Fortunately, there are endless resources online and in hard copy that can help you identify candidate schools.

1. Take a Sunday afternoon, turn off the TV, go to a bookstore, and find a big cushy chair. Bring a notebook and sit down with a stack of **COLLEGE GUIDANCE BOOKS**. Flip through the books and take notes on schools that interest you.

When you get home, check out the websites of the colleges you liked and discuss those schools with your parents. Also get input from teachers, coaches, and college guidance counselors.

2. There are numerous **COLLEGE SEARCH ENGINES** on the internet. These sites ask you to enter a number of variables—academics, location, size, cost, etcetera. Based on your entries, the search engine produces a list of matching schools.

Of course, you don't have to limit your college search to this computer-generated list. But it can be a good place to start.

At times, the volume of information on the internet is overwhelming, which is a strong argument for starting with a profile book, where the information is packaged in small, easy-to-access parcels.

COLLECT CONTACT INFO

Once you've found ten colleges that are right for you, use the internet to collect the contact information for each school and its soccer program. For each college, staple a single sheet of paper with the following information to a file folder.

SCHOOL_____

Location:

Size:

Web Address:

Conference:

COACH'S INFO:

Name:

Address:

Phone Number:

E-Mail:

Team Web Address:

7

GET ORGANIZED!

Being well-organized will simplify the self-recruiting process and make you more effective. Take the time now to organize yourself so that you can be systematic with the work ahead. Over the coming months, maintain your organization. As you take notes and receive literature, file everything carefully so it can be retrieved at a moment's notice.

SET UP A FILE SYSTEM

1. Get **10 FILE FOLDERS**, the kind with index tabs at the top.

2. **WRITE THE NAME** of one candidate school on the tab of each file folder.

3. On the front of each folder, **COPY THE CONTACT INFORMATION** you collected for your candidate schools, teams, and coaches (names, e-mail addresses, phone numbers, etc.)

4. **CREATE A LOG SHEET** *(see next page)* to help you record your progress. Staple one log sheet onto the inside cover of each folder. Add additional sheets later if necessary.

5. Go to each team's website and **PRINT THE ROSTER, SCHEDULE, AND GAME RESULTS TO HAVE AS REFERENCES.** Put the print-outs in your file folders.

FILE FOLDER UPKEEP

Throughout the process, **file all correspondence and literature in your folders**. Print e-mails you receive, and if you like, those you send. If you're really into it, photocopy letters and other correspondence that you mail hard-copy.

Self-recruiting is a lot like applying for a job in that when you communicate with a coach, **you should be knowledgeable about his team**. With the help of your folders, you will be able to discuss a team's schedule, roster, game results, and so forth.

By being well-organized, you'll equip yourself with the tools to talk with the coach about the upcoming game against the team's nemesis. You'll be able to ask about the recent nail-biter. And most importantly, you'll be able to knowledgeably discuss recruiting matters, like which roster positions will open up for your freshman season.

The coach will more than likely be impressed with your knowledge. **It will demonstrate your genuine interest in his team**.

Once you're organized, it's time to initiate contact with the college coaches you've identified. So take a deep breath and get ready to write a cover letter and soccer resume.

> Make sure the notes on your log sheets are dated correctly so at any point you can look through your file folders and see exactly what you've accomplished with each candidate school over a given period of time.

SAMPLE LOG SHEET

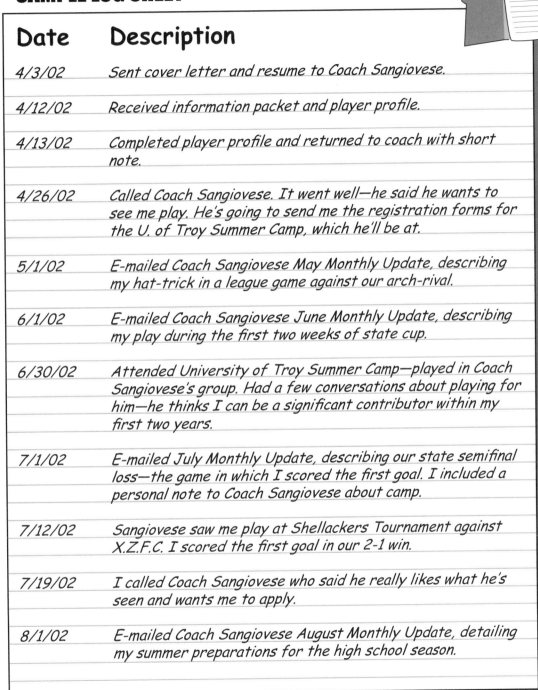

Date	Description
4/3/02	Sent cover letter and resume to Coach Sangiovese.
4/12/02	Received information packet and player profile.
4/13/02	Completed player profile and returned to coach with short note.
4/26/02	Called Coach Sangiovese. It went well—he said he wants to see me play. He's going to send me the registration forms for the U. of Troy Summer Camp, which he'll be at.
5/1/02	E-mailed Coach Sangiovese May Monthly Update, describing my hat-trick in a league game against our arch-rival.
6/1/02	E-mailed Coach Sangiovese June Monthly Update, describing my play during the first two weeks of state cup.
6/30/02	Attended University of Troy Summer Camp—played in Coach Sangiovese's group. Had a few conversations about playing for him—he thinks I can be a significant contributor within my first two years.
7/1/02	E-mailed July Monthly Update, describing our state semifinal loss—the game in which I scored the first goal. I included a personal note to Coach Sangiovese about camp.
7/12/02	Sangiovese saw me play at Shellackers Tournament against X.Z.F.C. I scored the first goal in our 2-1 win.
7/19/02	I called Coach Sangiovese who said he really likes what he's seen and wants me to apply.
8/1/02	E-mailed Coach Sangiovese August Monthly Update, detailing my summer preparations for the high school season.

PART III
OFF-FIELD SELF-RECRUITING:
INITIATING CONTACT

Regular communication will strengthen your cause and help you develop your relationship with a coach.

You demonstrate through letters, phone calls, and e-mails that you are committed to becoming a member of his team.

Give the coach a reason to seek you out specifically at a camp, tournament, or regular season game. Regular communication will put you in a position where he is eager to evaluate your ability.

8

COVER LETTER

The best way to initiate contact with a coach is with a personalized letter. Think about that euphoric feeling you have when you get an actual letter. You tear it open, feel the paper in your hands, unfold it, and flatten the creases with your thumbs. You read it once, maybe twice and analyze the signature. Alright, enough romanticism. The point is that coaches are human; they too like to receive mail.

SET A FOUNDATION

The first order of business is to send a cover letter and soccer resume *(see Chapter 9)* to the head coach at each of your candidate schools. **You want the coach to receive your letter and create a folder in his filing cabinet with your name on it.**

This cover letter will serve as the foundation of your marketing campaign.

Without overstating the importance of your letter, recognize that it **makes your first impression on the coach**. It should be a polished piece, organized and well-written. Avoid grammatical and spelling gaffes. Impress the coach with your attention to detail and professionalism.

Don't Start With A Phone Call Or E-mail

Do not begin your communication with a coach with a phone call. Unlike a letter, a call leaves no physical record. Remember, **self-recruiting is about doing the coach's work *for* him**. Present him with a written outline of your qualifications.

Don't make him write out the transcript of an introductory phone conversation—he probably won't anyway. In fact, he's likely to ask you to send him a cover letter and resume.

E-mail also should not be your first impression on a coach. Compared to a hard-copy letter, e-mail is rather impersonal. It is a fantastic tool for the later stages of self-recruiting, but it's not the right way to start.

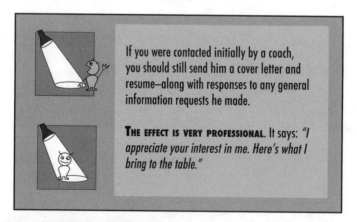

If you were contacted initially by a coach, you should still send him a cover letter and resume—along with responses to any general information requests he made.

THE EFFECT IS VERY PROFESSIONAL. It says: "*I appreciate your interest in me. Here's what I bring to the table.*"

WRITE YOUR OWN LETTER

The structures, content, and sample cover letters that follow are suggestions. Don't merely reword the examples. **The cover letter is an opportunity to express yourself**. It's a chance to showcase who you are.

Be concise. Remember that this is just an introduction, so avoid long-windedness. Your letter should be succinct—no more than one page—and informative.

Establish a tone within your letter to distinguish it from the mass of communication the coach has to sift through. Find the middle ground between over-the-top absurd and sleep-inducing. Don't be afraid to include personal details that distinguish you from the pack—i.e. *"I do my training runs at altitude, on Mount Olympus."*

If you're so inclined be playful, sincere, thoughtful, anecdotal, whatever. Just don't beg. You are an asset; a coach will be fortunate to have you as a player.

ORGANIZATION OF THE LETTER

LETTERHEAD	At the top of the page arrange your name, address, phone number, and e-mail. **EXPERIMENT WITH DIFFERENT FORMATTING AND FONTS UNTIL YOU FIND A STYLE THAT LOOKS GOOD.** Use this letterhead for all of your hard-copy correspondence throughout the self-recruiting process.
COACH'S ADDRESS	At the upper left, beneath your letterhead, write the coach's name and address in the font that you will use throughout the letter.
TODAY'S DATE	April 30, 1803—or whatever the case may be.
SALUTATION	Address each letter personally—i.e. *"Dear Coach Nascimento."* Form letters addressed *"To Whom it May Concern"* aren't worth the paper on which they're printed.
INTRODUCTION	State the intention of the letter, that you are interested in playing soccer for his team.
SELF-DESCRIPTION	Describe yourself as a player. Discuss your play on the field, what your tendencies are, and the responsibilities you have on team. If you're a team captain, say so. If you take the free kicks, and scored four of them during the high school season, say that too. If you will graduate in a different year from the rest of your club team, make it abundantly clear—i.e. *"Although I play for an '87 team, I will graduate a year earlier than most of my teammates."*
ACCOMPLISHMENTS	Briefly describe your qualifications and most recent awards. You don't have to list all of your accomplishments in your cover letter—that's what your soccer resume is for.

THE NEXT STEP

Promise to follow up on this initial inquiry with a schedule of your team's games and tournaments. In the meantime, request any standard recruiting materials. Most coaches have general information forms they like recruits to fill out. This helps streamline the deluge of information they receive from prospective players.

Indicate that a resume is attached. Let the coach know that you look forward to a response, and will be in touch soon.

CLOSING PHRASE

"Sincerely," "All the best," etc.

SIGNATURE

Your John Hancock.

YOUR NAME

Type your name beneath your signature.

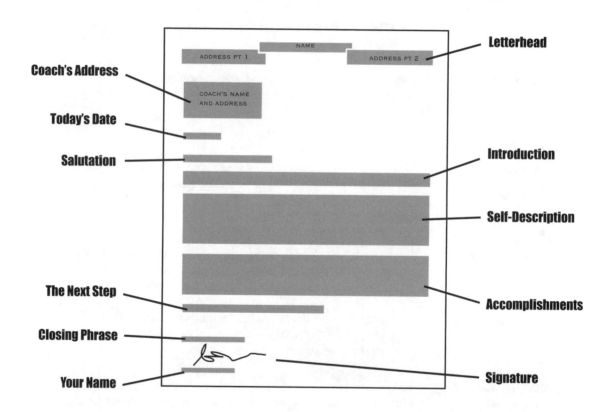

COVER LETTER PITFALLS

As much as your cover letter is an opportunity to be creative and to express yourself, you should keep it crisp, clean, and professional. Don't be self-indulgent and wander off on fifty different tangents. Say what you want to say in a succinct, articulate fashion.

The most common cover letter pitfalls are listed below.

 THINGS TO AVOID

Bragging	*"I will be the best player on your team. Give me a full scholarship and I'll score a bazillion goals."*
Putting Coaches To Sleep	*"I am very interested in being on your team which is a really, really good team at a college which is right for me because I am a pretty good student with a 3.3 GPA."* Zzzzzzzzzz. Nap time.
Begging	*"I know you're very, very busy, but if you can find the time, I would love for you to send me some information about your team."*
Asking For Too Much	*"I look forward to being flown out on an official recruiting visit."* Or, *"Please send one of your scouts to watch my game in Timbuktu."*
Clichés	*"In college, academics will be my first priority."* Coaches have heard that line a million times.
Stating Your Name	*"Dear Coach Firooz, My name is Chadwick Bugg and I am a senior at Tiberius Claudius High School in San Francisco, California."* Use your first sentence to state your purpose and attract the coach's attention. Your letterhead already says who you are.
Too Many "I's"	*"I am interested in your school. I would like to learn more about your team. I would like to come out and visit."* Don't begin every sentence or paragraph with the word "I."

Panky Q. Solari

14 South Beagle Street
Kalamazoo, MI 34676

psolari@slushies.org
(768) 534-3958

Coach Markus Olubisamoko
NESW University
134 Avenue Ln.
Hackensack, NJ 07601

8/3/03

Dear Coach Olubisamoko,

I am writing to express my interest in playing soccer for Northeast Southwest University.

This season I was the starting left-winger for the Nova High School girl's varsity, where I am a junior with a 3.4 GPA. Our drive to the state title fell short, as we lost in a semifinal barnburner to our rival high school. We were, however, district champions. To this campaign I contributed 5 goals and 11 assists. I was named to the district first team and state honorable mention.

During the club season I play forward for the Southside Slushpuppies, a team which regularly competes for the Michigan State Cup. Two years ago we won state and reached the quarterfinals at regionals.

As a player, I am at my best taking on defenders and going to goal. I spend a lot of time developing my foot skills. I pride myself as a hard worker and diligent defender. I am not the most vocal person on the field, but through my work ethic I maintain a position of respect on my team.

You will find my soccer resume attached to this letter. I am eager to learn more about your soccer program and coaching philosophy. As soon as decisions are made regarding our spring tournament plans, I will send you a schedule. In the meantime please send me any pertinent information regarding your team.

Sincerely,

P. Solari

Panky Solari

L. Clifton Buendia   234 Domain Street   cliff@milkyway.com
Range, WY 24375   345/375-2678

Tresorio Antonio
Univ. of the U.S.
1 Flag Drive
Concord, MA 26357

4/5/02

Dear Coach Antonio,

I've been researching colleges for the last few weeks and have identified the University of the United States as a school that could be a very good fit for me.

I carry a 3.1 GPA and am a member of the speech and debate team. Eventually I hope to go to law school. I am versatile on the soccer field, having played every position at some point over the past two years for Dry Lake High School.

If I have been a bit of a journeyman, it is partly the result of injuries that have plagued our team. Ideally I am a central defender/defensive midfield player. My coaches regularly compliment my vision and distribution, though they agree that my greatest strength is an ability to win defensive battles, especially 50/50 balls.

My club team, Marauders, plays in the competitive Range League, which is comprised of top teams in the region. For Marauders I generally play defensive midfield in a 4-4-2. I love getting forward on corners, and have scored on three such opportunities this season.

Fitness is a matter I take very seriously. I often run in the foothills of the Grand Tetons. Recently, I ran an 11:15 two miler. I love the game dearly and organize regular pick-up games during the off-season.

I have attached a resume of my academic and athletic achievements to this letter. I am excited about the possibility of playing for you and am looking forward to moving along with the application process. I will call your office late next week. I look forward to speaking with you.

All the best,

Clifton Buendia

READ THROUGH YOUR LETTER

Once you've written your letter, **read it out loud a few times** in different places around your house. Does it read smoothly? Does it sound like you? Have a friend, parent, or teacher read it and give you input.

As you read the letter, make revisions. It's a good idea to do a few drafts before you send it off.

STYLISTIC POINTERS

Look at your letter at arm's length and decide if you like the way it looks. **A coach will naturally pay more attention to a letter that looks readable**. A jumbled mass of text is unapproachable and will receive brief attention at best. So make your letter visually appealing.

Assess the overall appearance of your letter. Is it too busy? Is the font legible? Is the font size okay? Are the paragraphs too long or too short?

IMPROVE THE LOOK OF YOUR LETTER

- **BALANCE THE LETTERHEAD** size with the rest of the document. The letterhead should not "outweigh" the text.

- **USE A BASIC, READABLE FONT** like Times New Roman or Palatino. Don't use swirling, whirling calligraphy.

- **DON'T USE A HUGE FONT SIZE** to compensate for a short letter. 12 pt. font is usually the best size.

- **SKIP SPACES BETWEEN PARAGRAPHS**. Don't indent. This serves to space the text nicely, making the document more approachable.

- **AVOID MASSIVE PARAGRAPHS THAT INTIMIDATE THE READER**. Your paragraphs should be comprised of no more than four or five succinct sentences.

Once you have polished your cover letter it's time to roll up your sleeves and build a soccer resume.

9

SOCCER RESUME

Like your cover letter, a creative, well-organized soccer resume will help distinguish you from the pack. Your resume provides a quick reference and synopsis of your career. A coach can look over your resume and see that you've been playing position X for team Y for Z years. As soon as he looks at your resume, he begins to get an idea of what you're about.

You may actually find it easier to do your resume first and use it as a reference while writing your cover letter. Whatever order you prefer, attack the resume-building process with gusto!

RESUME COMPONENTS

PHOTOGRAPHS

School photos and especially **COLOR ACTION SHOTS** will energize your resume. Develop a design around your photos that's aesthetically pleasing. A coach will pay more attention to a well-designed resume and be more likely to remember it.

LETTERHEAD

If it fits your resume, you can simply use the letterhead you already designed. Otherwise, organize your name, address, phone number, and e-mail in a format that works well with your resume.

MEASUREMENTS

List your height and weight.

ACADEMICS

To receive a coach's serious consideration **YOU HAVE TO BE UP FRONT ABOUT YOUR GRADES.** Let him know from the start that you're up to snuff academically. Include GPA, SATs, ACTs, etc. Also include your year of graduation.

UNIFORM INFO

Include your club and high school uniform numbers, as well as home and away jersey colors.

SOCCER EXPERIENCE

STARTING WITH THE MOST RECENT, list your experience with high school and club teams. Describe your accomplishments, awards, positions, etc. Don't bother mentioning your U10 exploits. Concentrate on your recent history.

BE CONSISTENT WITH FORMATTING. The document should have a uniform overall appearance. Whether you choose to write in complete sentences or fragments, do so throughout.

OTHER INTERESTS

Demonstrate that you are not one-dimensional. In what other organizations, clubs, and activities have you participated?

REFERENCES

Ask at least two of your coaches to serve as references. On your resume, provide their names, telephone numbers, and e-mail addresses.

SEND IT OFF

Once you have polished your cover letter and resume, **get them in the mail right away**. Don't let them sit on your desk and gather dust. Print a cover letter and resume for each candidate school. Make sure the contact information is correct so the coach at school A doesn't receive a letter addressed to the coach at school B.

Address an envelope to each school. Sign your cover letter and fold it together with your resume. Stuff and stamp the envelopes, and get them in the mail.

Panky Q. Solari

14 South Beagle Street
Kalamazoo, MI 34676

psolari@slushies.org
(768) 534-3958

GENERAL INFO

Height: 5' 6"   Weight: 130   Left-footed

ACADEMICS

GPA: 3.7/4.0   SAT: 1240   ACT: 26
Graduate Spring 2005
Academic interests: Mortuary Sciences, Psychiatry.

SOCCER EXPERIENCE

Nova High School Varsity 2002-2003
Two-year letterman; 5 goals, 11 assists as a junior;
Started every game at left wing; 2003 All-State
honorable mention, District first team; 3 goals, 5
assists as sophomore. #9—White: home; Green: away.

Southside Slushpuppies 1998-2003
3-time State Cup winners: 2001, 1999, 1998;
Midwest Regionals quarterfinalist 2001; Starting
forward; 11 goals, 14 assists during 2003 season.
#14—Indigo: home; Red: away.

Michigan State Select 2001-2002
Two year selection to the state team;
Team finished third at Midwest Region
ODP camp, 2002; Played wing and forward.

REFERENCES

Amanda Mondraga; Head Coach, Nova High School
amon@nova.edu; (768) 876-9654

Salamadra Salchica; Head Coach, Slushpuppies
salasal@slushies.org; (768) 531-3546

INTERESTS

Hunting and gathering; Primitive tool collection;
Baroque choral singing.

L. Clifton Buendia

234 Domain Street
Range, WY 24375

cliff@milkyway.com
345/375-2678

Class of 2003
1140 SAT
6'0"
11:15 2-mile

3.1 GPA
23 ACT
165 lbs.

SOCCER EXPERIENCE:

Dry Lake High School: 2003 Wyoming AAA state runner-up; two-time varsity captain, 2002-2003; 2003 first team all-district; three-year letter winner; three-year starter; played sweeper and stopper; 2003 stats: 3 goals, 10 assists; uniform number 6.

'86 Marauders Soccer Club: Played for team since 1998; starting center-back since 2000; State Cup champions, 2001; winners: 2000 Vegas Invitational, 2001 CIA-KGB Cup, 2002 Surf's Up Cup; uniform number 10.

ACADEMIC INTERESTS:

Political Science, Pre-Law, Alchemy, Transmogrification.

EXTRACURRICULAR PURSUITS:

Senior Class President, Speech & Debate, Chess Club.

REFERENCES:

Chip Sedgwick, Head Coach, Dry Lake High School,
325/789-7568; chips@dlh.edu

Hugh G. Mongus, Head Coach, Marauders Soccer Club
325/345-6574; mongus@marsclub.com

10

FOLLOW-UP

Within a few weeks of sending out your cover letter and resume you will probably receive an information packet from the coach. The packet is likely to include literature about the team—newsletters, picture books, etc.—and a player profile sheet for you to complete and return.

Don't be put off if the response you receive is impersonal. It's not an indication of the coach's interest in you. It's simply a standard first response he's developed for solicitations from prospective players.

FILL OUT THE PROFILE AND SEND IT BACK

College coaches receive countless inquiries and cannot reply personally to everyone the first time around. If you are **persistent, you'll start getting some personal attention**.

Most coaches develop a player profile form so they can have a consistent reference for all of their recruits. **Think of this profile as the title page for your folder in the coach's filing cabinet**.

The information sheet also measures your interest level. Serious recruits are a self-selecting group. Those who are half-interested or half-committed usually fall by the wayside; they simply stop communicating with a coach.

When you receive the profile, **fill it out immediately, find an envelope and a stamp, and get the thing in the mail**. Don't promise to do it in a couple of days and then let it get lost on your desk under a pile of rubbish. A quick response will show that you are genuinely interested in the soccer program.

E-PROFILES

Some coaches will ask you to complete a profile on the team's website. If this is the case, do so immediately. Depending on the design of the website, completed electronic profiles may print as a jumble of responses interspersed with incoherent computer babble. Therefore, you should also print out a copy of the profile, fill it out by hand, and mail it in.

Accompanying Note

Instead of sending the player profile sheet back by itself, attach a brief note—or e-mail if you've done it online.

Type the note or jot it with a pen if your handwriting is legible. Use the same letterhead you developed for your initial letter whether you type or handwrite.

Demonstrate that you actually read through the materials. Let the coach know what you liked most—i.e. *"I got really excited reading the account of your run to the conference championship last year. Sounds like it was a thrill."*

Conclude by saying that you look forward to corresponding regularly throughout the recruiting process.

--HATTIE'S FARM COLLEGE--
PROSPECTIVE STUDENT-ATHLETE PROFILE

GENERAL INFORMATION

name_____   date of birth_____

address_____

home phone_____   e-mail_____

parents' names_____

ACADEMIC BACKGROUND

high school_____ graduation year_____

location_____ GPA_____ class rank___/_____

SAT I (math)_____ SAT I (verbal)_____ ACT_____ SAT II_____

academic awards, honors, leadership roles _____
areas of academic interest_____

other schools you are considering_____

ATHLETIC BACKGROUND

height_____ weight_____ other sports played_____

club team_____ uniform color/number_____/_____
position_____ awards_____
coach_____ phone number_____

high school team_____ uniform color/number_____/_____
position_____ awards_____
coach_____ phone number_____

years of odp_____ highest level reached (state, regional, national)_____

return this form to: coach ann toine-meyer
country rd. 35-agraria, pa 62135 – 347/345-7456 – toine@thefarm.edu

SAMPLE ACCOMPANYING NOTE

FABIANA ABRAXIS

14 NORTH STREET
ATHENS, GA 21954

FABIANA@DOLOMITE.ORG
(412) 634-3478

9/1/03

Dear Coach Toine-Meyer,

Thank you very much for the information regarding women's soccer at Hattie's Farm College. It sounds like you've got a great group of girls.

I was particularly impressed with what the newsletter said about the victory against your rival, University of the Atlantic Ocean, after having lost three games in a row.

Having read through your information packet a few times, I am really excited about playing for Hattie's Farm. From what I know of the school, I think it will be a great fit for me.

For now, I have completed the player profile form, which you will find attached to this letter. I will be in touch with you soon.

Sincerely,

Fabiana Abraxis

Instead of saying vaguely that *"I will be in touch with you soon,"* feel free to be more specific by indicating that you'll call the coach next week, or that a schedule of your team's tournament appearances is on the way.

NEWSPAPER CLIPPINGS

Clippings from local newspapers are a nice additional touch. It's a bonus for the college coach. If a newspaper has written about you, send a photocopy of the article along with your completed player profile and accompanying note. Highlight the parts of the article that are about you.

PACKET BUT NO PROFILE

Some coaches' information packets do not include player profile sheets. If the packet you receive doesn't include a player profile, you should **still respond promptly**.

Immediately e-mail the coach to acknowledge your receipt of his mailing. Your e-mail should be similar to the accompanying note described previously.

Let the coach know that you have read through the literature he sent. Mention your favorite details—i.e. *"It sounds like you had a great pre-season trip to Sri Lanka."*

Indicate that you are eager to move forward with recruiting, and that you will call or e-mail again in the near future.

IF THERE'S NO RESPONSE
TO YOUR COVER LETTER AND RESUME

If a month passes and you don't hear from a coach, **don't frrrreak out and convince yourself that he's not interested**.

Gather your wits and write him a brief e-mail explaining who you are and what you sent him. Ask if he received your letter, and if there is a general information sheet you should fill out.

To:	baltazar@stc.edu
From:	Sally Maltus <sallymander@theswamp.org>
Date:	April 7, 2008 10:05:00 EST
Subj:	Sally Maltus Cover Letter & Resume

Dear Coach Baltazar,

I recently mailed you a cover letter and resume indicating my interest in playing soccer for Sands of Time College. Please let me know if you received and have had a chance to review my letter.

I am very excited about the prospect of playing for you and want to take all the necessary steps to show you that I am right for your team. If you have general prospective player forms and standard literature regarding the soccer program please send it my way.

I'm very eager to hear from you!

Sincerely,

Sally Maltus

Still No Response

If you send your e-mail and a week passes with no response, it's time to give the coach a call. Pick up the phone and dial. Be forthright with the coach: ask him to clarify why it is that you haven't gotten any response.

CALL TO CLARIFY

You may be totally smitten with a particular school even though you haven't gotten much of a response from the coach. If this is the case, and you decide to be very persistent, you should CALL THE COACH TO FIGURE OUT WHAT'S GOING ON.

Here are some things you might want to say during that phone call:

- *"Hi Coach Del Piero. This is Tati Francesca from Naples High in Florida. I recently sent you a cover letter and resume. I haven't heard back from you, so I decided to give you a call to make sure that you received my stuff."*

- *"I'm very interested in your school and I'd love to play for your soccer team. At this point I just want to get a sense of whether I should continue pursuing a spot on the team."*

- *"I'd really like to arrange an occasion on which you can see me play in person. How should we go about doing that? What else can I do at this point to show you that I'm right for your team?"*

He may say that he's been very busy and has had little time to work on recruiting—in which case **you've probably done yourself a great service** by calling him. You've advanced your cause and done his work for him.

On the other hand, the coach may say that frankly he really doesn't think that you are right for his team. If this is the case, you have two options:

- It's quite possible that he's made up his mind. Still, if you are really interested in this school you can be persistent and urge him to see you play before he writes you off. Be careful about expending too much energy on it. This could be a dead end.

- Alternatively, you can let this school fall by the wayside and say to yourself, *"Alright, this is probably not going to work out. I'm going to concentrate instead on the five schools whose coaches responded positively to my cover letter and resume."*

SET A HIGH STANDARD

The quality of your early contact with a coach sets the standard for your recruitment. To be effective, the tone of your cover letter and follow-up information must demonstrate *enthusiasm and determination.*

Without being in his ear 24/7, show the coach that you are committed to making this happen. If you slack off, it will be perceived as disinterest. So stay with it.

PART IV
OFF-FIELD SELF-RECRUITING:
MAINTAINING CONTACT

Once you've gotten through to your candidate coaches **you must maintain regular contact with them**. Until you've joined a team you cannot stop corresponding with the coach.

If you have the right academic and athletic credentials **there is nothing more important to recruiting than regular communication**. It sends a clear signal that you're serious about this. It also gives a coach the opportunity to really get to know you.

The best ways to develop your relationships with college coaches are phone calls, e-mails, and letters.

11

PHONE CALLS

Once you've sent a coach your cover letter and resume, and have replied to all requests for supplemental information, it's time to buckle down and get on the horn.

Phone calls from college coaches have an exaggerated reputation, as if once you've been called you're assured a spot on the team. Many high school players also mistakenly believe that if they don't receive a phone call the situation is hopeless.

There are countless reasons why a coach may not call you—**many of which do not reflect your ability to play for his team**. This is what makes self-recruiting so important. **Doing things like making phone calls will strengthen your cause.** Don't just wait for calls to come to you. If you do sit and wait, the calls may never come.

LIMITING FACTORS

Each coach has his own phone calling philosophy. Some call recruits weekly, others monthly. Still others never call, opting for written correspondence or for the player to call them. If this is the case, what a pity it would be if you never picked up the phone!

You'll quickly get a sense of what mode of communication works best with a particular coach. As these trends emerge, **make notes in your file folders outlining the best ways to be in touch with each coach**.

NCAA regulations are also a factor. If you're a junior making a mad dash for the phone every time it rings, stop sweating. The NCAA prohibits coaches from calling recruits before July 1st of their senior year of high school. **But that doesn't mean that as a sophomore or junior you can't call them**.

Sophomores and especially juniors should speak with coaches on the phone. The call, however, has to be on your dime. A coach is **not even allowed to return a message** from a recruit before July 1st of the recruit's senior year. So if you leave a message and receive no response, keep calling until you eventually connect with the coach.

COMMON MISCONCEPTIONS

- Recruiting phone calls are only for coaches to make.

- One call from a coach means that you're guaranteed a spot on the team.

- No calls from any coaches means nobody wants you.

- Calling a coach is something to be really nervous about.

WHEN TO CALL

Be conscientious about when you call coaches. Don't call on Friday at 5:00 PM or two hours before the team has a game. Consult each team's schedule, which you should have in your file folders. **Mornings are often the best time to call coaches**, because they're not in a rush to get to practice.

Since you're probably in school at this time, you need to develop a calling strategy. Some high schools allow students to make long distance calls to colleges on school phones. Otherwise, use a cell phone or buy a calling card that you can use at a pay phone.

Give A Heads-Up

It's a good idea to **inform a coach that you are going to call him**. E-mail him a day in advance so he can review your materials before you talk. That said, you shouldn't expect him to know your resume by heart.

To:	msoc@southie.edu
From:	Inukshuk Johnson <nunavut@cairn.com>
Date:	November 11, 1998
Subj:	Phone call tomorrow

Dear Coach,

I trust that you have received my completed player profile by now. I'm as enthusiastic as ever about the prospect of playing for your team. I am eager to speak with you about my prospects with the team and how to progress with the recruiting process. Tomorrow I have a free period from 9:30-10:15 EST during which I will call your office.

Until then,

Inukshuk Johnson

1 DAY LATER...

Take a deep breath and dial with confidence. Remember, **you're doing the coach's job for him**. Be assertive when you call; make it a conversation, a two-way exchange of information.

Nothing is worse for both parties than an awkward silence that deteriorates into a cross-examination by the coach. This is a conversation, not an interrogation.

Before you call, **consult your file folders to refresh your memory about the team**—what conference they play in, how many seniors are on the team, what their record is this season, who they play next, the roster positions they need to fill, etc.

Make a list of discussion topics, pleasantries and substance alike, so the conversation doesn't stall. Cross 'em off as you go.

Be frank with the coach. Ask general questions about the soccer program and what you need to do at this point to distinguish yourself from his pack of prospective players.

PHONE PREPARATION

Sample questions progressing from lighter to more serious:

- *How is the current season going?*

- *What system are you playing?*

- *I see you're graduating 6 seniors—where on the field will you need the most help in the coming years?*

- *Have you had time to review my cover letter and resume?* If he hasn't, **BE PREPARED TO OFFER A BRIEF ORAL RESUME.**

- *Do I have the kind of soccer background that you look for in prospective players?*

- *At this point, what can I do to further my case?*

When you hang up, breath deeply again. Phew, it wasn't so bad, right? Take a moment to **jot down your impressions of the call**—personal tidbits about the coach, the program, where you think you stand, and what steps you need to take next. File your notes and record the call on your log sheet. Now repeat the process for your other candidate schools.

MORE CALLS

Beyond this ice-breaker phone call, you should **call each of your candidate coaches from time to time**.

How often you should call depends on a number of variables, including how far out you are from graduating, your application plans, whether you're trying to coordinate a visit or a tournament appearance, etc.

Generally speaking, **you should call a coach every couple months**. As application deadlines near, or as you plan a visit, you may need to call more often.

WHEN A COACH CALLS YOU

If a coach calls you, **be an active participant on the phone**. Don't just sit there and receive a lecture. Think on your feet—ask questions, make observations. At the end of the call, thank the coach for taking the time to call you. Let him know that you will be in touch in the near future.

If you self-recruit well, as a senior you will start receiving phone calls from your candidate coaches. Your work will have begun to put you in the recruiting spotlight. **This does not mean, however, that you should stop calling the coaches**.

You should definitely reciprocate from time to time. It's a great way to raise your standing. In other words, if a coach has been calling you, a call *from you* will leave him feeling very positive about your recruitment.

12

THE POWER OF E-MAIL

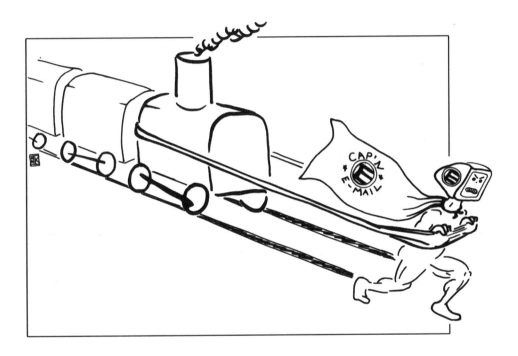

E-mail is a recruiting asset with unlimited potential. It is a medium of informal, succinct, and rapid correspondence. Use e-mail to its fullest **to develop and maintain dialogues with your candidate coaches**.

Some coaches are incredibly e-mail savvy. If a coach is sitting at his desk when you send an e-mail, you might receive an immediate response. Be forewarned that there are also some coaches who are e-mail illiterate.

INFORMAL E-MAIL EXCHANGES

If e-mail proves to be an effective tool with a particular coach, maximize its potential throughout the recruiting process. **Update coaches regularly on your successes on the field and the status of your application**.

Respond promptly to e-mails that they send you. When you receive an e-mail from a coach, hit reply and write a few paragraphs. Don't let it sit unanswered for days on end.

Have rapid-fire e-mail conversations with coaches; **encourage them to have casual back-and-forths with you**. Don't agonize over the wording of your e-mails, which should be informal, yet respectful. They don't have to be as polished as your cover letter.

In sum, use e-mail to its full potential. Without spamming coaches, keep them posted on your accomplishments and application progress. This will demonstrate that you are reliable and committed.

GET ON THE NET

If you're e-mail illiterate, now is the time to change. E-mail will prove indispensable throughout self-recruiting—not to mention when you're in college, where e-mail is a way of life.

Set up an e-mail account separate from your parents. Get comfortable at the keyboard and start e-mailing coaches.

SAMPLE INFORMAL E-MAIL

To:	tpaine@cmnsns.edu
From:	Marquis Cummerbatch <granmarquis@jade.calm>
Date:	September 25, 2004 9:00pm
Subj:	Thanksgiving, etc.

Dear Coach Paine,

Thanks for jotting me that e-mail the other day. It sounds like your season is going quite well.

I thought I'd let you know that I scored in a game this weekend against our cross-town rival, Shackleton High School. They've got some great players, including a few of my club teammates. It was fun going up against them in front of the whole school. In the end we lost 3-2, but there was frantic action until the final whistle.

Also, I want to let you know that it looks like my club team will be going to the Tofu Thanksgiving Tournament in Phoenix. Is there any chance that you'll be there? My team will only have a few weeks to prepare since the high school state tournament doesn't end until early November, so our Thanksgiving showing will be interesting...

Thanks again for your e-mail. I'll be in touch soon.

Marquis

REGULAR E-MAIL UPDATES

In addition to your informal e-mails with a coach, you should develop a **monthly e-mail update** so each coach knows that he's going to hear from you every four weeks. Use a playful, memorable, and descriptive title like **"Socorro LaFortune's First Monday Report"** for your update. Coaches know that they will hear from Ms. LaFortune on the first Monday of every month.

Effort like this will not go unappreciated by college coaches. Regular contact like this demonstrates genuine interest, determination, as well as dependability—traits that coaches value immensely. A creative marketing pitch of this sort will significantly improve your chances of making the team.

SAMPLE MONTHLY E-MAIL UPDATE

To:	deuschen@trampolineu.edu
From:	Mark Santorini <pyroclastic@juneau.ak>
Date:	June 1, 2004 11:11pm
Subj:	**MARK'S SIDEKICK**: Monthly Soccer Dispatch for the Month of June, 2004

Dear Coach Deuschenschlag,

I hope all is well with you. The weather here in Juneau has finally cleared, and we have more than three hours of daylight.

My team Yeti F.C. spent the last month training and competing on an indoor field-turf pitch 20 minutes from my house. We were aching to play outside when the fair weather finally arrived.

The last few sunny weeks have brought good fortunes to the team, as we have advanced to the State Cup final four. Last Saturday we won the State quarterfinal 3-1. We went down 1-0, and I scored the tying goal from right wing. Hopefully things will go well this coming weekend. If we win the title, we'll be at Far West Regionals in Albuquerque, NM. I hope to see you there!

As for my recruiting status, please let me know if there is anything further I can do at this point. You have a copy of our tournament schedule—I will let you know as soon as the exact details are available. Regionals aside, our next tournament near you is the San Diego Pipeline Cup in August.

Also, my teammate's father has been videotaping our games. Depending on the quality of the filming, I'll try to have a video to you within the next month.

That's it for now.

All the best,

Mark Santorini

One E-mail Update Will Work For Every Coach

An e-mail update like the one on the previous page is personalized enough to get a coach's attention. Meanwhile, **it's generic enough to work for the coach at each of your candidate schools**. You don't have to spend eons writing ten different e-mails. A single update—which you can write in an hour—can be e-mailed to every candidate coach.

—WARNING!

It's fine to add details to your update that are specific to a particular candidate school. Just make sure you don't accidentally send to College B what you intended for the coach at College A!

13

SCHEDULE OF APPEARANCES

As soon as the information is available to you, send each coach a well-formatted schedule of your games and tournaments. **If you begin self-recruiting late in your junior year or during your senior year, send your schedule along with your cover letter and resume.** You need to get things moving quickly.

GAME & TOURNAMENT SCHEDULE

College soccer budgets are stretched so thin that you simply can't expect a coach to make an enormous effort to see you play. Recruiting funds are limited and therefore guarded tightly. Coaches try to make the recruiting buck go as far as possible.

Translation: **the odds of a coach journeying cross-country to watch an isolated regular season game are slim**. Coaches who attend individual club and high school games probably represent local colleges—which may be fine with you if you're interested in them.

For colleges beyond your immediate vicinity, **you're far more likely to gain exposure at a tournament**— preferred by coaches because they can assess numerous prospects at once. In fact if you give a coach advance notice about a particular tournament, you might spark his interest in attending.

If a coach saw you play and then contacted you, determine the importance of being evaluated again. Does he want to reassess your play? Ask him over the phone or via e-mail.

Provide him with your appearance schedule regardless of his answer. Even if he doesn't need to see you play again, a schedule will give him a sense of the games and tournaments you're playing.

Type Your Schedule

Gather all the information you have regarding your team's schedule. Sit down at the computer and—**using the same letterhead** you developed for your cover letter and resume—cobble together a schedule. **Don't fret if you don't yet know the exact game schedule at a particular tournament. For now, just let coaches know that you're going to be at the tournament**. You'll pass on further details when they're available.

- **IF YOU SEND THE SCHEDULE AS AN E-MAIL,** do so as an attachment. This improves the chances that the coach will see the schedule the way you want it to appear—not as some fickle e-mail program displays it.

  Be careful about using unusual fonts. The coach's computer may not have those fonts, in which case all of your pretty formatting will revert to a generic font. Stick to the basic fonts like Times New Roman, Helvetica, etc. In the e-mail text field write a brief note explaining the schedule.

- **IF YOU OPT FOR SNAIL MAIL,** accompany your schedule with a note that also includes your letterhead.

SAMPLE SCHEDULE

Zorbas Shove
34667 W. Swamp Dr.
E. Rutherford, NJ 19837
zorkaj@scovjfam.org
201-447-8563

MEADOWLANDS PEARL DIVERS F.C.
UNIFORM COLORS: BEIGE AND MAGENTA; NUMBER: 7

TOURNAMENT SCHEDULE, FALL 2005

PLUTO CUP, DOLGEVILLE, VA - AUGUST 12-14

9/12	VS. GAWKERS FC	9:00 AM	FIELD 3
9/12	VS. BLOCKERS UNITED	4:30 PM	FIELD 6
9/13	VS. SHOCKERS '86	10:00 AM	FIELD 14
9/14	SEMIFINAL	9:00 AM	FIELD 2
9/14	FINAL	4:00 PM	FIELD 1

SEDNA CUP, SOUTH SHORE, NJ - OCTOBER 20-21

SCHEDULE TBA

BEETLEJUICE CLASSIC, MIAMI, FL - DECEMBER 4-7

SCHEDULE TBA

REGULAR SEASON SCHEDULE, FALL 2005

ALL GAMES AT MEADOWLANDS SOCCER COMPLEX

9/6	VS. F.C. COHO	11:00 AM
9/13	SEE ABOVE	
9/20	VS. SUPERDOME F.C.	9:00 AM
9/27	VS. ONION BREATH S.C.	10:30 AM
10/3	VS. MINOTAUR '87	2:30 PM
10/10	VS. FUCHSIA FOOTERS	9:00 AM
10/17	VS. CABBAGE PATCH '86	12:00 PM
10/24	VS. TURNPIKE F.C.	4:00 PM

SAMPLE ACCOMPANYING NOTE

Zorbas Shove
34667 W. Swamp Dr.
E. Rutherford, NJ 19837
zorkaj@scovjfam.org
201-447-8563

7/5/05

Dear Coach Jajonji,

Attached you will find a copy of my club schedule for the fall season. As you're on the other side of the country, I recognize that it is unlikely that you will be able to attend a regular season game. I've listed our league schedule anyway, just to give you a sense of the competition I get on a regular basis.

As far as tournaments go, we're going to play in the Pluto Cup, Sedna Cup, and Beetlejuice Classic. Are you planning to attend any of those events?

I'm really looking forward to the Pluto Cup next month. We finished second last year. This go around, we're playing our nemesis, the Shockers—who we lost to in last year's final—in the first round.

As soon as I have details on the other two tournaments, I will send them your way. I'll also call you soon to see if you're planning to be at any of these tournaments.

All the best,

Zorbas

 FAQ

What if I identify an additional college and team of interest when I have already made a lot of progress with my original candidate schools?

Say you've been diligently self-recruiting for five months. Your mother's friend comes over for dinner and talks up her alma mater. If you're convinced, all you have to do is a little catch-up work for that school.

Fortunately, you have your cover letter and resume saved on your computer. That very night, print out a copy of each, stuff them in an envelope, and have it postmarked and ready for the next day's mail.

14

REFERENCES

Enlist your high school and club coaches—the same people you provided as references on your resume—to write letters of recommendation for you. A positive evaluation from a credible high school or club coach will bolster your standing with college coaches.

PEOPLE YOU SHOULD USE AS REFERENCES

The coaches most qualified to provide credible evaluations of your ability are those who have known you for a while. Try to avoid using coaches who have known you for less than a full season.

Additionally, **try to get your recommendations from experienced coaches**. An experienced coach can say things in your recommendation like, *"In my 15 years of coaching high school girls, I haven't seen a better distributor of the ball."*

A parent or teacher who stands in as the coach of a team often cannot provide the soccer insight that college coaches seek in a reference.

If you have no alternative, it's not the end of the world. Any coach can at least provide general observations on your role within the team and personality traits like leadership and reliability.

> If you go to a college summer camp, **THOSE COLLEGE COACHES ARE OFTEN WILLING TO SERVE AS REFERENCES.** Recommendations from other college coaches can really strengthen your campaign.
>
> **ASK YOUR COACH FROM SUMMER CAMP TO WRITE AN EVALUATION** that you can send to your candidate coaches.

PREPARATIONS

Make your recommenders' lives easy by providing them with addressed and stamped envelopes to encourage them to get their letters off in a timely manner. Ask them to send their letters directly to the college coaches.

In your next e-mail update, **inform the college coaches that they should be expecting your recommendations**. Briefly describe who the recommenders are and how long you have played for them. **Mention anything else that strengthens their credibility**—did they play soccer in college or the English Premier League; have they coached ODP or at the college level?

FOLLOW-UP

Check with your recommenders after a week or so to make sure that they have written and sent the letters. If they haven't done it yet, gently urge them to do so. Keep checking back until they've done their job.

5 STEPS TO GETTING REFERENCES WRITTEN

1. Ask your high school and club coaches to write recommendations for you.

2. Get a stack of standard envelopes.

3. For each recommender, address one envelope to each candidate coach. Stamp the envelopes.

4. Give the envelopes to your recommenders. Ask them to send their recommendations ASAP.

5. Follow up with your recommenders a week later to make sure they've done their job.

15

VIDEO

Before you're offered a spot on a college team, the coach will usually want to see you play in person.

A highlights video is not a substitute for seeing you play in person. It is, however, a good way to **convince the coach to come see you play**. In sending a coach a video, you're just trying to whet his appetite—to distinguish yourself as someone he should seek out.

In having your play evaluated, **highlight videos are useful, but overrated**. Whether or not you make a video usually won't make or break your campaign. **It's just another tool that you provide a coach to help him make an informed decision**.

Many of the videos coaches receive are garbage anyway. Some videos look like they've been filmed during a cataclysmic earthquake. If it's not that, often the quality of the video is so grainy that players are little more than blurs on the screen. Some are sleep inducing. Others are downright painful.

A video of poor quality will not further your cause. Unless you feel like you can produce a video with quality footage, don't waste your time or certainly your money on a production company. If a coach requests a video and you can't provide something decent, let him know.

If he's adamant, send him what you've got, maybe with a little disclaimer. Let him know if you feel that what you're sending is inadequate and doesn't do your play justice. At least he knows what he's getting into.

When you send a video, your name, jersey number, phone number, address, and e-mail should always appear prominently on the DVD or video cassette.

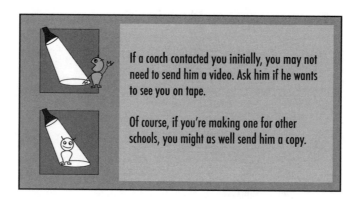

If a coach contacted you initially, you may not need to send him a video. Ask him if he wants to see you on tape.

Of course, if you're making one for other schools, you might as well send him a copy.

HOMEMADE vs. HOLLYWOOD

I'm not a big fan of professionally produced videos. I prefer it when players show the initiative, creativity, and wherewithal to do these things themselves. Anyhow, the 300 bucks you drop on a production company could just as well be put towards a digital video camera.

Kudos if you choose to do your own video. Maybe find a friend to work with. Put two VCRs side-by-side, review film on one, and splice it onto the other. Personalize your video as you see fit. Soundtracks, for example, are a nice personal touch.

Digital Video

Digital video is a great alternative to VHS. It is high resolution and relatively easy to edit. If you have access to a digital camera and a tripod, have someone film a game, practice, or pick-up session. Find a computer with movie software. Then craft your swanky little video.

Camera Angle

When filming, **the camera's distance from the field is very important**. Super close-ups don't show the context in which plays develop. Excessively wide-range shots come across as one big smudge on the TV. Find the average.

WHAT TO PUT ON YOUR VIDEO

Better, more enjoyable videos tend to start with a brief introduction and an explanation of how the viewer can identify the player on the screen. After that, it's on to the action footage.

Introduction

Take a minute at the beginning of the tape to **introduce yourself**. Speak clearly, confidently, *and enthusiastically* into the camera.

Don't be afraid to distinguish yourself from the pack with a few personal details like, *"My favorite animal is the kangaroo,"* or *"I am an avid collector of beetles,"* or *"I like the sound of subway brakes."*

Be enthusiastic and willing to smile. Players tend to be overly serious on their videos. You don't have to be giddy like the local weatherman, but coaches want real, vibrant, dynamic people, not automatons.

Identification

Figure out how the coach will be able to identify you on the screen. **Your best bet is probably your jersey number, if it's legible**. If you can't create titles on the screen, describe in the introduction how you can be identified throughout the tape. Beyond your jersey number, mention the position you play so the viewer knows where to look. **You might also have the filmer give some play-by-play commentary, just to clarify when you have the ball**.

Other distinguishing features can be useful such as alternate shirt colors, outlandish hairstyles, silver boots, whatever. Just make sure that the coach can pick you out when he watches the video.

Action Footage

There are two schools of thought when it comes to the actual content of a recruiting video. Most coaches prefer edited clips. Yet there are a few who like to watch recruits' games in full.

If most of your candidate coaches are asking for a short highlight video, you'll know which format to use. You can also be diplomatic and incorporate elements of each.

HIGHLIGHTS

If you choose to do a highlight reel, **make sure the video clips are shown in context**. In other words, don't just show yourself making a good pass. Show the build-up to the pass.

Employ the 2-3 Second Rule: **show 2-3 seconds of play before and after the highlight**. The coach wants to see how the play developed and how you were involved throughout.

NOT EVERY CLIP HAS TO BE A GOAL

Many high school players mistakenly believe that they should only put goals on their videos.

Actually, **YOU SHOULD INCORPORATE ALL SORTS OF CLIPS IN YOUR VIDEO**. Even if the outcome is not heroic, clips of you defending, dribbling, passing, and moving in space can be useful for a coach.

If you made a really nice run in which you won a tackle and then beat a defender, only to have your shot blocked, don't disregard the clip.

College coaches are well aware that not every play ends with a goal.

RUN-OF-PLAY

If you have access to high-quality video in which you are easily distinguished and featured regularly, you might prefer to utilize a more free-running, extended play format. Run-of-play videos can incorporate anything from five-minute unedited clips to an entire 45-minute half.

Don't show run-of-play action if you are only recognizable in the frame once every ten minutes. Watching such a video is a waste of the coach's time; he'll lose interest very quickly.

SMALL-SIDED GAMES

PRACTICE OR PICK-UP GAMES CAN PROVIDE EXCELLENT ACTION FOOTAGE. In the setting of a small-sided game, you get a lot of touches and the camera isn't flying all over the place. Unlike a full-field game, the action and off-the-ball movement of a small-sided game can be captured simultaneously on tape.

Put your fears to rest if you're concerned that a coach will think a pick-up or practice game is "rigged." Just get out with a group of your friends and play.

A COLLEGE COACH IS CONCERNED WITH HOW YOU MOVE AND PLAY. A video with high-quality footage of a small-sided game can show a coach what he needs to see.

LENGTH

A highlight reel shouldn't last longer than ten minutes. After your 10,000th goalasso, it becomes tiresome.

Run-of-play videos can feature 10-20 minute uninterrupted spans, or last an entire half. Whether a coach will watch it all is another matter. But at least extended play is available if he's inclined to watch.

If you use extended, run-of-play footage, **provide a key** that identifies you and your role at specific times on the video. Do at least a little editing, by cutting out footage when you're not on the field. **Keep the total running time under 45 minutes**.

SAMPLE VIDEO KEY

SOSHY KAY SMITH

5 Manatee Way	336-457-1435
Boca Raton, FL 25478	soshy@thesmithy.com

VIDEO KEY

Video length: 38 minutes

Jersey Number: 19—The one with the red ponytail!

Position: Left-Wing

00:00:00	*Introduction.*
00:01:24	*Highlights.*
00:05:35	*Game starts.*
00:13:43	*My shot goes off the cross-bar.*
00:15:22	*1-on-1 sequence.*
00:23:42	*Left-footed cross.*
00:25:12	*I play a long ball which results in a goal.*
00:30:17	*A big tackle!*
00:32:23	*Little give-&-go.*
00:34:14	*Right-footed shot from 25-yards.*
00:37:45	*I clear the ball off our line.*

VIDEO FORMATS

VHS

VHS is a fail-proof platform for your video. If a coach can't access a video in VHS format, he needs to stop gnawing that wooly mammoth bone and leave the stone age.

CD-ROM

Avoid using CD-ROMs because they are often impossible for coaches' computers to access. It's simply a waste if a coach attempts to watch your video on his computer, but for some formatting reason can't open the thing. If you have no alternative to CD-ROM, include specific instructions on how to access the video—what program to open it with and so forth.

DVD

DVDs are the best digital format for your video. Most DVD players will happily play your video. An added perk of a DVD is the size. After watching your video, a coach can put it in the file he has for you, so all your information is stored together.

 —WARNING!—

No matter what video format you choose, give your video a test run to make sure it works before sending it off.

PART V

ON-FIELD SELF-RECRUITING:
APPEARANCES

Your **performance on the field**, as much as your dedicated correspondence, will convince a coach that you deserve a spot on his team.

Your regular contact thus far will have sparked his interest in personally evaluating your ability. The key now is to **arrange a time and place for him to see you play**.

Though on-field self-recruiting is all about actual appearances, even now **you must maintain the dialogue** that you've established with a coach.

You've worked so hard to get his attention. Don't disappear now. **Don't lose his attention by abandoning your telephone and e-mail campaign**.

16

ON-FIELD APPEARANCES

You can't judge a prospective player by his soccer resume. Coaches know that on the field, players aren't necessarily what they appear to be on paper. Seldom is anyone offered a spot on a college team just because his or her resume looks good. Your letters, e-mails, and phone calls cannot tell the whole tale.

Finding a way for a coach to evaluate your play in person is critical. You may be attractive on paper and a brilliant phone conversationalist. In the end, however, most coaches will want to see you in action before they include you in their long-term plans.

Effective communication, therefore, lays the foundation—off-field self-recruiting motivates coaches to see you in action, on the field.

Imagine a college coach at a tournament with 24 teams and 413 anonymous players. Such probabilities do not favor the players. But if you've self-recruited well, that **coach knows that he needs to single *you* out of the crowd**. In fact, he's made a note to see you play in your 2:30 game.

Off-field self-recruiting will put you in the spotlight and tilt the odds of being seen in your favor.

SUMMER CAMPS

Many college soccer programs run summer camps, which are an ideal setting for coaches to evaluate prospective players. You may attend as many camps as you like, all of which must be at your own expense. The NCAA prohibits college teams from paying recruits' camp fees.

Summer camps are often run at a host school and feature coaches from a number of different colleges. **Camps provide an unrivaled opportunity for coaches to thoroughly evaluate prospective players**—and likewise, for players to assess the coaches.

Players are usually divided into teams that are headed by one college coach. Over the course of the week, though, the players will have the opportunity to work with every other coach. In this forum players can be examined at length, so that a few bad touches in an isolated game don't define your play in the eyes of a coach.

Beyond your extensive exposure to a coach on the field, **camps allow players to develop personal relationships with coaches**. In passing, in the cafeteria, and at scheduled extracurricular activities, you will be able to have casual conversations with them.

You can also arrange to eat lunch together or meet in the dorm lounge if you'd like to speak with a coach more formally about your college prospects. Just don't be overbearing by constantly requesting to meet with a coach.

Making Arrangements & What To Do Once You're At Camp

During the winter of your junior year, **ask your candidate coaches which camps they intend to work that summer**. They may even volunteer this information unsolicited in an effort to get their recruits to a venue where they can be observed extensively. Once you know the camps a coach will attend, make the appropriate notes on your log sheets. Request the camps' promotional materials and registration forms.

After having a few such conversations with various coaches, you might determine that the coaches from, say, your seven schools of greatest interest will not be attending any camps in common. **Fortunately, college coaches are highly networked and are often willing to share information about prospective players**.

At some camps, the staff will write college recommendations for all of their campers. At other camps, you may have to ask. Some coaches will even make calls on your behalf to candidate coaches who were not in attendance at the camp.

When you're at a college summer camp, use it as an opportunity to talk to the coaches you're interested in playing for. **Schedule a time to speak with them 1-on-1**—maybe in the dorms or cafeteria. Ask each coach his impressions of your play, and whether he envisions a role for you on his team. Discuss the aspects of your game you should work on to contribute to his program.

The camp staff will often feature active college players, many of whom spend the summer on campus working or taking classes. **Utilize these players as resources**. Talk to them. What is college soccer really like? What kind of commitment does it entail? What are their impressions of the coaches you're courting?

> Say you decide to attend the X University Soccer Camp—a school that interests you. You're also enthusiastic about A College and B University, whose coaches will not be at the camp.
>
> In this case, ask the coaches at A College and B University if they know any of the coaches at the X University camp who can evaluate you on behalf of A College and B University.

Camp Tuition

Unfortunately, college camps are expensive, often costing more than $500 for one week. Soften the financial blow by thinking of camp as a sound investment, one that offers the most thorough exposure to college coaches.

WARNING!

Camps tend to fill up very quickly. Some of the most popular camps are fully booked as early as February. So early on, consult a calendar to plot out the camps you need to attend. Call the camps to request registration forms and then send them off right away.

TOURNAMENTS

Tournaments provide an excellent opportunity for coaches to get a glimpse of you in a competitive environment. Though coaches' exposure to you may not be as intensive and thorough as in a camp environment, perceptive coaches can get a sense of your play pretty quickly.

To successfully arrange for a coach to see you at a tournament, **provide him with a schedule**, as described in Chapter 13. **As soon as you know your team's general tournament plans, let coaches know**—i.e. *"We're going to Wanderer's Cup in January and The Explorer Invitational in March."* E-mail the coach the exact game schedule when the details are finalized.

If a coach you've contacted is in attendance at a tournament, don't freak out thinking that you have to hog the ball and score seven goals to make your case. Relax and play as you normally would.

In fact, you probably won't know when exactly the coach is watching. Concern yourself with playing the game, not with scanning the crowd for a guy wearing Bananaville University yellow.

 **PARENTS**

Before you go to a tournament, make a bunch of copies of your child's team roster. The roster should include each player's name, jersey number, address, phone number, e-mail, grades, SAT & ACT scores, and year of graduation.

While the team is playing, walk around and distribute the roster to the college coaches that are watching—they won't be hard to identify. The whole team will benefit from this. If you run into one of your child's candidate coaches, feel free to chat briefly with him.

GET COACHES TO COME TO YOUR TOURNAMENTS

Don't be afraid to lobby a coach to come see you play at a specific tournament. Convince him that this is a tournament he should really come watch. E-mail him little teasers like:

"We have a very competitive schedule at the Prometheus Invitational. Based on past experiences, I think this will be a fantastic tournament to watch. It would be great if you could come."

INDIVIDUAL GAMES

It's unlikely that college coaches will attend isolated high school or league games unless signing you is an absolute priority or you play close to the college.

If these conditions aren't working in your favor, you should still provide coaches with a schedule of your regular season games—if for no other reason than to show them that you are playing regularly.

KNOW WHEN YOU'RE BEING EVALUATED

Ask each coach which tournaments or individual games he's going to attend. Though he may not have his schedule figured out exactly, he might be able to give you a general idea. This isn't so that you can honor him with an extra-special effort on that extra-special day. It's so you know what games he's seen and when to **have follow-up conversations regarding your play**. Take notes on your follow-up conversations and how you think you played while he was watching you.

You should be aware that NCAA regulations stipulate that coaches cannot speak with recruits before, during, or between games. College coaches also may not speak with recruits until the club or high school coach has released the players at the end of a game.

17

ON-FIELD APPEARANCES
FOLLOW-UP

A college coach may hang around after the game to speak with you. If you see him from afar and he hasn't found you, **walk over and introduce yourself**. Don't be intimidated or throw yourself at his feet. Just have a normal conversation. Offer your opinion of the game, ask for his, thank him for coming, and promise to be in touch.

SEND AN E-MAIL

Whether or not you manage to talk to the coach immediately after the game, **make sure to contact him the following week**. Send him a thank you e-mail for making the effort to see you play. Offer some analysis of the game and indicate that you are eager to move forward with recruiting and your application. Ask briefly for his impressions of your play.

Your follow-up e-mail should be short and informal. Yet it should move your dialogue with the coach towards the critical issue of where you stand.

You've been in regular contact now with the coach for months. He's reviewed your cover letter, resume, and video, and seen you play in person. **You need to start figuring out if he truly foresees a role for you on his team**—i.e. if he will offer you a spot on the pre-season roster.

To:	shak@sonora.edu
From:	Ariel Mitbar <ari@desert.com>
Date:	Feb. 27, 2003
Subj:	This past weekend, and the future...

Dear Coach Shakahaji,

Thank you very much for taking the time to watch me play this past weekend. I was pretty happy with my play. I admit that I was a little rusty, having been restricted to playing indoors for the last few months. As a team, we feel that it was a good start to our spring season.

I really do appreciate you making the effort to see me play. It's been a pleasure corresponding with you over the last eight months and getting a sense of what your team is all about.

From our correspondence—letters, e-mail, and phone calls—I think you've probably gotten a sense of me personally. Now that you've seen me play as well, I'm looking forward to discussing the prospects of playing for your team. I'll be in touch soon.

All the best,

Ariel Mitbar

FEEDBACK

If you did a good job initially matching your academic and athletic credentials with candidate schools, **it's likely that after being evaluated on the field you will begin to hear some positive feedback**.

You may indeed have received enthusiastic responses from coaches well before they saw you play in person. If you have been committed to self-recruiting, your regular correspondence has probably turned the spotlight in your direction, setting you apart from the pack of prospective players.

If your candidate coaches haven't voluntarily shared their feelings about you as a recruit you'll have to ask them. Through more e-mails and phone calls you'll get the feedback you need to determine which schools you should continue to pursue and which you should dismiss.

PART VI

DELIBERATION, NEGOTIATION & MAKING A DECISION

Decision time is fast approaching. You've been in regular contact with coaches. They've seen you play and have heard from your references.

You've provided them with everything they need to make an informed decision about you.

You must now find out what that decision is. **Of your candidate coaches, who foresees a role for you on his team**?

From the coaches who respond favorably, you have to then decide whose schools you will apply to, and ultimately which one will provide you with the best overall experience.

18

DECISIVE CONVERSATIONS

Once you have put yourself in the spotlight and have given a coach a strong sense of you personally and as player, it's time to **request his honest opinion of your chances with his team**.

DON'T AVOID THE DIFFICULT QUESTIONS

Recruiting boils down to a rather simple equation:

> College coaches want qualified student-athletes.
>
> - AND -
>
> You want to be identified as such a person.

As you continue to correspond with your candidate coaches, **don't lose sight of the ultimate goal—that you want to be identified as a player who's right for the team**. It's fine to have informal conversations with coaches, but don't dance around the central issue. Now is the time to be straightforward and determine where you stand.

Don't expect a coach to simply volunteer that you are one of his top recruits. If he does, great. If not, you shouldn't think that you are out of luck. **You must be assertive and find out how serious he is about you**.

When To Have These Conversations

You should have decisive conversations once you are well into the self-recruiting process. Before you go asking for an assessment, give the coach plenty of time to review your cover letter and resume, check your references, and see you play. A thorough coach will want the full picture before he decides to bring you onto the team.

Once you are convinced that the coach has a thorough sense of you, call or e-mail him. Phrase your questions in a genuine, non-confrontational fashion. **The most important thing is that you actually bring up the subject of your standing**. You're asking perfectly reasonable questions; there's no reason to be shy about this.

CANDID DISCUSSIONS

As you approach the impending decision of where to apply **you need to have a clear understanding of your prospects with each team**. A few targeted questions will shed light on your standing with a coach.

These questions and associated topics should be discussed and elaborated upon over the course of a few e-mails and phone calls. You don't have to slam him with one epic barrage of questions. Get a general sense of how he regards you, and then iron out the details over the following weeks.

Call Or E-mail

To discuss your standing with a coach, choose between e-mail, with which you can articulate yourself more deliberately, and a phone call, which is more personalized. **Take into consideration the mode of communication that has been most effective with each coach**.

If e-mail has worked better with a particular coach, go with it. If you've had greater success calling that coach, use the phone.

If you choose to write an e-mail, incorporate the following questions without writing a laundry list of thirty-seven million numbered questions.

SAMPLE QUESTIONS TO ASK

- *"Now that you've seen me play twice and have spoken with my high school coach, how do you think I can fit in with your team?"*

- If the coach responds with something vague like, *"I think that over time you can contribute,"* ask for more specifics.

- *"Will you offer me a spot on the pre-season roster, or will I have to walk on?"*

- *"Do you think I can contribute immediately—can I get playing time as a freshman? Or do you envision me seeing very limited playing time for the first few years? If so, what's your Red Shirt policy?"*

- *"Is there athletic scholarship money that will be available for me? How are scholarships spread among the team?"*

- *"What's your relationship like with the admissions department? If I apply, what kind of assistance can you offer in terms of moving my application favorably through admissions? Will you support my application?"*

- Mention to the coach if you've begun to narrow down your field of candidate schools. If his school is one of your top two or three, let him know.

- **BE FRANK WITH THE COACH OF YOUR TOP CHOICE**— *"Under the Sea College is without a doubt my top choice. If I am accepted and offered a spot on the soccer team I will definitely come."*

To:	olidubi@oohooh.edu
From:	Buckwheat Rios <buckie@wheat.grn>
Date:	June 19, 2005
Subj:	Recruiting Standing

Dear Coach Olisadibuo,

Thanks again for watching my game two weeks ago at the Sahara Invitational. Things could certainly have gone better for us, but I imagine you got a decent sense of my play.

I am very excited about the prospect of playing soccer for you at Ugasd University. Having seen me play, I'm interested to hear what role you envision for me on your team. First and foremost, I'd like to know where I stand among your recruits for next year.

Will you be able to offer me a roster spot, as a recruit, immediately? What kind of contribution do you think I can make as a freshman, and throughout my time at U.U.?

As for admissions, if I apply do you intend to support my application? For that matter, what do you think are my chances of being admitted? If admitted, would an athletic scholarship be available for me?

Though I'm still deliberating over a few details, I want to be clear that U.U. is definitely one of my top three choices. I'm very enthusiastic about U.U.'s academic and extracurricular opportunities and, of course, about the soccer team as well.

In general, I'd like to know how you think I can fit in with your team and plans for the future. I'm very excited to hear back from you on these issues.

All the best,

Buckwheat Rios

GUARANTEED POSITIONS & PLAYING TIME

While you're having these decisive conversations be wary of hollow promises. A coach might try to woo you by dangling the guarantee of a starting position.

Remember that **he still hasn't seen you play with his team**. He can't be certain how you'll fit in with the team and adapt to the college game. You may be a latter day Pele on your club team but require development to be effective at the college level.

From your end, don't press coaches for such guarantees. Instead of going on the offensive and asking a coach to assure you the role of starting center midfielder, phrase the question in a more general, and less confrontational fashion: *"What would you say are my chances for playing time as a freshman at center midfield?"*

Self-recruiting is about getting yourself onto a college team where you can eventually contribute. Actually **earning minutes on the field is something you have to do when you arrive on campus**. If you want playing time as a freshman, you have to prove yourself during pre-season.

FOLLOW-UP E-MAIL

After you've sorted out your standing with a coach and determined that he wants you on his team, you should ask him how exactly to proceed. Figure out what steps you need to take to apply to the college, get your financial aid/scholarship situation in order, and meet eligibility requirements.

To:	reuben@xyzu.edu
From:	Renata Limon <lemon@de.com>
Date:	August 1, 2005
Subj:	The next step

Dear Coach Reuben,

After our recent series of conversations I'm more excited than ever about playing for XYZ University. Thank you so much for your interest in having me on your team. From our correspondence over the last few months and my overnight stay with Angie I have a very positive impression of the team.

At this point, I want to do everything I can to make sure that it works out. What steps do I/we need to take to make sure that I am admitted? I know that you've said that you would support my application. From my end of the table, what do you suggest I do to strengthen my application?

As far as paying for college, I know that your team doesn't offer athletic scholarships. In sorting out how to pay for school, are there specific people in the financial aid office who have been particularly helpful in the past? Who should my parents and I speak with?

I just want to say again that I am very excited about the prospect of playing for your team. Thank you again for all of your help over the last few months.

Sincerely,

Renata Limon

What if the coach at a candidate school tells me that under no circumstances does he see a place for me on his team?

Unfortunately, responses of this sort are not unusual. It's what inevitably happens when you try to funnel a few hundred thousand high school players into the college ranks, which can only accommodate a few thousand players.

This statistic is small consolation; rejections are bound to sting. Such an outcome may wound your pride, but don't let it shatter your confidence.

Don't give up your hopes just because one coach doesn't have a place for you on his team. Throw away the file folder for that school and focus your self-recruiting efforts on the teams that remain.

If at the outset of self-recruiting you found ten or so teams that matched your ability, by the end you should have at least one or two coaches who want you to play for them.

19

SCHOLARSHIPS

Many players and parents mistakenly believe that if you can't win a scholarship you can't play college soccer. The reality is that **the majority of college soccer players do not have athletic scholarships**. Demand is way too high and supply is way too low.

Put simply, there are far more college soccer players than there are college soccer scholarships.

ATHLETIC SCHOLARSHIPS

Unless you're one of the top players in the country, don't expect a team to give you a *full athletic scholarship*. There are even some college players with national team experience who aren't on full rides.

For scholarship-worthy recruits, *partial scholarships* are more likely. College coaches are strictly limited to a certain number of total scholarships. Being a very frugal breed, coaches often divide their scholarships among a number of players.

If you are not offered an athletic scholarship, don't give up your college soccer dreams. Nor should you necessarily remove a candidate school from the running because you are not offered an athletic scholarship.

> **If a coach doesn't offer me a scholarship, does that mean he doesn't want me on his team?**
>
> **No**. Year in and out this myth races through circles of players and parents. It has been the downfall of many college soccer careers before they even begin. **DON'T BE DETERRED IF YOU AREN'T OFFERED A SCHOLARSHIP.**
>
> The reality is that between dramatic legal and financial restrictions, college teams are very limited in their ability to pay their players' tuition. Does that mean that you might not get an athletic scholarship? Possibly. Does it necessarily mean that a coach doesn't want you on his team? No.

When An Athletic Scholarship Is Not Available

Many schools don't even offer athletic scholarships. There are no scholarships in the prestigious Ivy League nor in the entirety of Division III.

Schools that do offer athletic scholarships are strictly limited by the NCAA to a certain number of scholarships. Whether a school actually funds the full allotment of scholarships is another factor that can work against you.

When it comes to tuition, there are usually payment alternatives. You and your parents just have to be creative and persistent.

Never write off a college for financial reasons without consulting the school's financial aid office. With the financial aid people, discuss academic scholarships, minority scholarships, community service scholarships, federal grants, and loans.

Scholarship Limitations

In a given year, a Division I women's soccer team is allowed a total of twelve scholarships. The coach can divide those twelve scholarships among as many players as she wishes. So twelve players may get full scholarships, or 24 players might get half scholarships. **Coaches tend to choose the latter course, dividing scholarships among a number of players**.

As mentioned before, a college may offer athletic scholarships, but not *fully fund* the NCAA/NAIA allowance. So there are Division I women's teams out there that only have, say, eight scholarships.

When you factor in the 25-person roster of a college team, the outlook for a full scholarship for the average player is rather bleak.

Early Research

In your early correspondence with coaches, **determine what kind of scholarship money might theoretically be available for you**.

SCHOLARSHIPS ALLOWED

	Women's Teams	Men's Teams
NCAA Division I	12	9.9
NCAA Division II	9.9	9.0
NCAA Division III	none	none
NAIA	12	12

Find out the size of the scholarship pools from which you'd be drawing. Determine if your candidate teams are fully funded—i.e. if a Division II team you're investigating has the full allotment of 9.0 scholarships.

This can be a strong indicator of a school's financial commitment to the soccer team and of the team's commitment to you. It says a lot if a team is offering you a 75% scholarship out of its pool of four total scholarships.

Spend some time taking detailed notes on your scholarship outlook with each candidate team. File the notes in your folders.

A coach who is committed to getting a recruit will often investigate the recruit's chances of getting institutional financial aid. If the team was going to offer the recruit a 50% scholarship, but the college will offer a 60% scholarship, it makes sense to go the non-athletic financial aid route.

Later In The Process...

Once you are well into the self-recruiting process and the coach at a candidate school **has a strong sense of your ability, discuss your scholarship outlook more specifically**. Build on your discussions from Chapter 18, where you determined how serious each candidate coach is about getting you on his team.

Ask the coach if he will offer you an athletic scholarship—and in what amount. Assess the offer, and what it means your family will have to pay.

To:	juarez@pojoaque.edu
From:	Zzack Andriopoulos <zack@z.com>
Date:	October 9, 2004
Subj:	Scholarships

Dear Coach Juarez,

I was thrilled to find out the other day that I am one of your top recruits. Thanks for the huge vote of confidence! I'm quite certain at this point that I'm going to apply.

Amidst all the excitement, my parents and I are trying to figure out how to finance my college education. You and I had that phone conversation a few weeks ago regarding athletic scholarships. I know you said that you expect to be able to offer me a scholarship, though you didn't specify the exact amount.

I recognize that you only have six scholarships to divide among the entire team. Any scholarship money you can offer me is greatly appreciated.

As my parents and I try to work through this whole paying for college thing, an estimate of the soccer scholarship I should expect will really help.

I look forward to hearing from you.

Sincerely,

Zzack

THE RULES OF ATHLETIC SCHOLARSHIPS

There are many rules that govern athletic scholarships. If you're offered a scholarship, go to the NCAA's website and familiarize yourself with some of the rules.

Download a copy of the *NCAA Guide for the College-Bound Student-Athlete*. Learning about scholarships will prevent you from following dead-end leads and breaking rules that endanger your eligibility.

- **ATHLETIC SCHOLARSHIPS ARE NOT GUARANTEED FOR FOUR YEARS.** They are awarded one academic year at a time for up to five years. So sometimes a player will get a scholarship one year and not the next.

  Coaches are usually considerate about keeping injured players on scholarship. However, before signing with a team, you should ask the coach how he deals with injured players who are on scholarship. If you get injured and have to sit out a year, will you lose your scholarship?

- Division III schools **DO NOT OFFER ATHLETIC SCHOLARSHIPS.** Non-athletic scholarships, however, are often available on the basis of academic excellence, extracurricular talents, and demonstrated need.

- Pell Grants and other **GOVERNMENTAL SCHOLARSHIP** programs may be available in addition to athletic scholarships. Contact individual admissions departments to learn more about such opportunities and whether you can mix athletic scholarships and institutional financial aid.

  (Source: NCAA Guide for the College-Bound Student-Athlete - www.ncaa.org)

NON-ATHLETIC SCHOLARSHIPS

Institutional financial aid is available at many schools as need-based, academic, minority, and departmental scholarships—to name a few categories.

These awards are a great way to deal with the skyrocketing tuition of many schools, though competition for this money is intense. At each candidate school, **research the non-athletic scholarship opportunities through the admissions department and financial aid office**.

Questionable Scholarships

In recent years some colleges have found loopholes in NCAA regulations. They offer murky "leadership" or "activities" scholarships that allow them to circumvent NCAA bylaws.

Think long and hard if you're offered a sketchy scholarship. Discuss its legality with the coach, admissions department, and perhaps even a lawyer. If the NCAA determines that it is a violation, you could lose your eligibility.

FREE APPLICATION FOR FEDERAL STUDENT AID (FAFSA)

There are a number of federal college scholarship funds and programs, including Pell Grants, low-interest government loans, and Federal Work Study. To apply for these funds, you have to start with the FAFSA.

The FAFSA is basically a family finances questionnaire. Based on your responses, the Department of Education produces a Student Aid Report which includes your *Expected Family Contribution (EFC.)*

This report is made available to you and the colleges to which you apply. Schools use your EFC to determine if you should receive federal financial aid, and the form in which it should be—loans, grants, etc.

For more information, and to complete the FAFSA online, visit:

www.fafsa.ed.gov

 **PARENTS**

Making financial arrangements for college is intimidating for high school students. Parents can be a tremendous help by contacting admissions and financial aid departments and working through the financial aspect.

In your conversations with a school's financial aid people, try to devise a solution to the essential question: **IF MY CHILD REALLY WANTS TO GO TO YOUR SCHOOL, WHAT DO WE NEED TO DO TO MAKE IT HAPPEN?**

The answer may not come easily, but don't tear out your hair. Work towards the answer systematically, with the guidance of the admissions department. Keep in mind that **IF THEY ACCEPT YOUR CHILD, IT'S BECAUSE THEY WANT HER TO ACTUALLY COME TO THEIR SCHOOL.**

20

CAMPUS VISIT

A campus visit is an essential component of determining which college is right for you. **It is your opportunity to get a sense of the school and the soccer team first-hand**. A campus visit is also a great piece of self-recruiting: it vividly demonstrates your interest in a team.

If you self-recruit well, the coach at a candidate school will ask you to come visit. **If he doesn't ask, you should volunteer**. Let him know that you'd like to come see the place.

It's preferable to visit once the coach has a pretty clear sense of you personally and as a player. The best time for most recruits is during the fall of your senior year—once you're well into the self-recruiting process and are poised to actually apply.

If your schedule demands that you visit before he has seen you play, it's not the end of the world. At the very least, before you start making major travel plans, the coach should have your cover letter and resume. You should also gauge his interest.

VISIT YOUR TOP SCHOOLS

Unless you're willing to shuttle all over the place, visiting your original ten candidate schools will probably not be feasible.

By now, you've probably cut your candidate pool down to five or six schools. If not, **before you break the bank visiting them all, evaluate each school and try to narrow the field**. Look over your notes and review your impressions. Assess the quality of feedback you've received from each school.

Visit the candidate schools that you determine are best suited for you. Don't be afraid to let a few of the less appealing schools fall by the wayside.

OFFICIAL VISITS

If you've self-recruited well, you will be asked to come on an *official visit* during the fall of your senior year. Such visits are paid for by the team—**meals, admissions to campus athletic events, and transportation may be paid out of team funds**.

With the exception of top recruits at top Division I teams, it's unlikely that the team will pay your travel expenses. Soccer teams' budgets are already stretched thin. So don't worry if a coach doesn't offer to pay for your transportation. You should be willing to get yourself there.

NO ATTENTION

If at this late stage in the recruiting process a coach is inattentive, you should seriously assess the likelihood of playing for that school. Be honest with yourself—does playing for that team seem realistic?

Then again, if you're determined to play soccer in college, you cannot fold at the slightest sign of adversity. Who knows, a coach may just be disorganized, overwhelmed with work, or even bluffing a bit to see how committed you really are.

If you still want to play at a school where you haven't received much of a response, don't write it off before you've had an honest discussion with the coach.

DON'T BE AFRAID TO PRESS THE COACH FOR AN EXPLANATION. Does he think that you're qualified for his team? As a recruit? As a walk-on?

If the answers to these questions are not favorable, move on and concentrate on your remaining candidate schools.

THE RULES OF VISITING

Strict NCAA guidelines govern official visits. You should familiarize yourself with the rules before making any visiting commitments. A few of the most important rules are listed below. The *NCAA Guide for the College-Bound Student-Athlete* describes the rules in greater detail.

- Recruits are LIMITED TO **5** OFFICIAL VISITS.

- Only **1** OFFICIAL VISIT may be made AT EACH SCHOOL.

- Official visits may ONLY OCCUR DURING A RECRUIT'S SENIOR YEAR of high school.

UNOFFICIAL VISITS

Before your senior year, all visits are unofficial. You must pay all of your expenses, including travel, meals, and admissions to athletic events. These visits are great to do during the spring of your junior year to get a feel for a campus. **You may make as many unofficial visits to a campus as you like.**

If a coach doesn't offer you an official visit as a senior, you should evaluate your prospects with that school. It may be an indication that you are not high on the coach's recruiting board.

Nonetheless, if you're deeply interested in that school, consider visiting unofficially. **Though the visit may be unofficial, you should still try to coordinate it with the coach**. He may assist you with arranging transportation from the airport and organizing an overnight stay.

You should simultaneously coordinate your unofficial visit through the college admissions department, which can provide you with meals and housing without violating NCAA rules.

UNANNOUNCED VISITS

The circumstances of your visit may be different from those described above. You might take a whirlwind 20-day, 16-state college trip during the summer, when no one is on campus. Or, you might be at a college for an academic or music summer program.

Whatever the circumstances, **e-mail or call in advance to arrange to meet the coach while you're on campus**. If for some reason you can't give advanced warning, find the coach's office and knock on the door.

ON CAMPUS AT LONG LAST

You may arrive for your visit and find an itinerary awaiting you. Don't be freaked out if you aren't given a hero's welcome. Some coaches roll out the red carpet for recruits. Others require you to be more self-sufficient. Face it, there are also some coaches who just aren't organized well enough to put together a detailed schedule for you.

Some coaches provide transportation to and from the airport. Make airport pick-up arrangements before your trip, so you don't have to spend the night on the baggage carousel.

While you're on campus, keep in mind that **this is an opportunity for you to evaluate the school and soccer program**. You have a lot of say in this decision. As much as you're trying to woo the coach, so too must his school and soccer program demonstrate their worthiness. If you don't like a college, **you don't have to go there just because the coach wants you to come**.

Most importantly, **recognize that this is your potential team for the next four years**. Do you like what you see in terms of style, quality of play and instruction, the team's attitude on the field, as well as the social dynamic?

There are many components to a successful visit. Whether or not an itinerary has been made for your visit, while you're on campus you should meet with the coach, watch a game or practice, and stay overnight with a player.

Meet With The Coach

There's no substitute for a face-to-face discussion with the coach. Arrange a time during your stay to drop by his office for a chat.

As with the phone calls described in Chapters 11 and 18, prepare yourself with questions you want to ask. Don't feel burdened by having to start the conversation with the difficult questions concerning your standing.

Instead, be prepared to start with a lighthearted chat about your stay, your current high school season, whatever. Most coaches want to get a sense of you on a personal level—as you should of them.

 **PARENTS**

If you visit with your child, **DON'T DOMINATE THE CONVERSATION WITH THE COACH**. It's fine to contribute, but don't monopolize the spotlight and reduce your child to a disengaged third wheel, squirming in the corner.

If your kid is quiet, ask some questions that will provoke his input and get him involved in the conversation.

Steer the conversation towards more substantive fare—namely your position within the coach's recruiting class. Be persistent without being aggressive, by asking something to the effect of, *"Honestly, where do you feel I can fit in with your team?"* This question represents the essence of recruiting, and must not be avoided just because it's a little uncomfortable.

Reference and build upon earlier conversations you had regarding your standing—i.e. *"I know that you've said that you would bring me onto the pre-season roster. Do you think that I can be a significant contributor as a freshman?"* **Try to leave his office with a clear understanding of your prospects with the team**.

See A Game

When planning a campus visit, consult the team's schedule—which you have in one of your file folders. If possible, **schedule your visit to coincide with a college home game**.

Watch the game with a critical eye. Among other reasons, the coach might ask you later for your impressions! Figure out what formation the team plays and what its tactical tendencies are.

- What players impress you? Are you eager to play with anyone in particular?

- Do you think your play will fit well with the team, in terms of talent and style?

- Do you like the way the coach interacts with his players, opponents, and officials?

Watch Practice

Observing a practice can be as valuable as watching a game. If you schedule your visit for a couple of days that include a game, you'll probably be able to watch practice as well.

During practice, resist the temptation of mindlessly juggling a ball or watching the southern migration of Canadian Geese. Pay attention to the practice and imagine yourself participating.

- Are the drills useful? Enjoyable?

- Is the team enthusiastic about practicing? Do they work hard? Do they have fun?

- How well is practice organized? Does practice have a theme, or does it just go from one drill to the next?

- How does the coach give instructions? Is he positive and encouraging or negative and belittling?

Stay Overnight With A Player

Staying overnight with a player on the team is a great experience. It will provide insight towards the college at large, the social dynamics of the team, and the players' true esteem for their coach. It's also just downright fun.

Staying with a player will **give you a sense of what college life is like and what the team does off the soccer field**. Ask questions of as many players as possible.

Find out how they balance schoolwork and soccer. What do the players do on the weekends? Do they live together? Are they in fraternities? Do they socialize only with soccer players and other athletes?

Ask them about the coach's style and what they think of practices and game management. The players are a resource for honest answers to your questions about the school. **If selecting a college and soccer program all over again, would they make the same choice**?

Finally, if you enjoy your stay and make good personal connections, **get the players' e-mail addresses** so that you can contact them directly if you have any further questions. When you get home, put all of this contact information in your file folders.

FOLLOW-UP

Take notes immediately after visiting a school. You may forget some details after a couple of days, so write down your impressions while they are still fresh in your memory.

10/12/05

Just returned from visit to Gondwanaland University. Had an excellent overnight stay with Winford Mizner, a talkative sophomore center fullback - wmizner@gndwnlnd.edu. Met most of the team, all of whom seem very friendly. Team watches movies and plays a lot of whiffle-ball together. I think I could fit in very well.

I really like Coach Pangea. He thinks that I will be able to help the team as a freshman - he thinks I'll get significant playing time, probably on the left wing.

The campus is incredible. Students are always out in the main quad studying, throwing frisbees, etc. It seems like there's a lot going on.

The classes I sat in on were interesting. The economics professor was pretty dull compared to the animated geology professor.

The team's game was a bit disappointing. They didn't play very well and lost 2-1. The quality of practice was much higher - it was clear that these guys are good players. I think it would be a good setting for me as a player.

Thank The Coach

Send a thank you e-mail to the coach. Let him know that you enjoyed your visit, staying with the team, and watching the match.

Thank the coach for taking the time to meet with you. If you forgot to ask him a question during your meeting, ask now. Finally, let him know that you're excited about moving forward with the recruiting and application process.

To:	thenicki@estrn.edu
From:	Thaddeus Finneran <thadd@olivebranch.com>
Date:	September 30, 2002
Subj:	Great Visit to Eastern

Dear Coach Hodnicki,

Thanks for helping me organize my visit to Eastern this past weekend. The result in Saturday's game was unfortunate, but I enjoyed watching the team nonetheless. Waylon was a great host. We had a great time on campus and downtown on Saturday night.

I'm glad that you and I had the opportunity to meet in your office. The meeting shed much light on the soccer program and what it's like to be a student-athlete at Eastern. I have a quick question that I meant to ask during the meeting:

How are professors about accommodating players' soccer-related absences? In other words, if I miss an assignment or a test because I'm on the road with the team, will I be able to make it up? Or will I be penalized?

Overall, the visit really strengthened the case for Eastern. Having been there now, I'm almost certain that it will be a great fit. I hope you had an equally favorable impression of my stay.

I'll be in touch soon,

Thaddeus Finneran

Thank Your Host

You should also send a thank you e-mail to the player who hosted you. Let him know that you really appreciate him having taken the time to show you around campus and introduce you to the team. **Your host is a great connection to have in case you have additional questions down the road that you want to ask a player**.

More importantly, your host could be your teammate in the near future. Now is a great time to start building a new friendship. That way you'll have a confidant when you arrive on campus.

To:	waylon@estrn.edu
From:	Thaddeus Finneran <thadd@olivebranch.com>
Date:	September 30, 2002
Subj:	Eastern Visit

Waylon,

I just wanted to drop you an e-mail and say thanks for hosting me this weekend. As you warned, the couch was small, but comfortable enough! I had a great time seeing the city and watching the street performances downtown on Saturday night. Thanks for getting the team together so I could meet everyone.

I know you were disappointed with the game on Saturday. For what it's worth, I thought the team played well. I would love to be out there with you next year.

Thanks again for hosting me.

Thadd

What if I decide at some point during the recruiting process that a given school or soccer program is not right for me? How do I bow out gracefully?

After extended, favorable contact with a coach, you might visit a school only to discover that it has all the appeal of a medieval dungeon.

BE DECISIVE BUT CONSIDERATE IF YOU DECIDE THAT YOU'RE NOT INTERESTED. Let the coach know. You don't have to make a hullabaloo over it, or explain in depth what you didn't like. Write a quick e-mail, explaining that after further consideration, you've decided the school does not represent an appropriate choice for you. Thank him for his time and wish him well. Move on.

21

APPLICATIONS & ADMISSIONS

Once you've decided to apply to a school, call the coach immediately and let him know your intentions. Don't be emotionless—show that you are excited.

Few college coaches can simply snap their fingers and have a recruit accepted. However, **coaches who are effective recruiters have strong ties with admissions departments**.

The arrangements are different for each school, but most colleges have a system where **coaches identify and prioritize their recruits for the admissions department**. The coach might also write a blurb about each recruit and indicate his expectations of the player.

TYPICAL ADMISSIONS DESIGNATIONS

- Blue Chip—An immediate impact player.

- Will contribute as a freshman.

- Can contribute within a few years.

- Likely walk-on.

- Long-shot—Athletically, a real stretch.

Keep coaches updated on your application progress. Drop the coach an e-mail to tell him that you stayed up until midnight the night before putting the finishing touches on your essay. Tell him that you took the SATs again and scored fifty points higher. Let him know if you're going to apply *Early Decision*.

When you finally send in your application, e-mail the coach immediately so that he has a written record of it. Also remind him of your conversations regarding admissions—i.e. *"I know you said that you can't guarantee admission but that you would strongly endorse my application—at this point, what does that exactly consist of? I really appreciate any help you can offer."*

If you've self-recruited well, you will be in a position where the coach will support your application.

I've heard that being recruited to play soccer at a college guarantees admission to that school. Will my athletic ability allow me to get around the school's academic standards?

Being a recruited athlete rarely opens the admissions door if you don't measure up academically. If a coach knows that your academic record is sub-par, it's unlikely that he'll make a stand for you with admissions.

Coaches know that standing up for academically unqualified recruits usually fails. It also weakens the coach's credibility with the admissions department. An admissions department will be apprehensive of a coach who brings academically unqualified recruits to the table.

INDICATE YOUR TOP CHOICE

If the coach at your favorite candidate school wants you on his team, **a potent way to strengthen your application is to let him know that his school is your top choice**. He will pass that information on to the admissions department.

The blurb he writes about you for the admissions department might say something to the effect of, *"Kyle will definitely come if he is admitted."* A phrase like that pleases admissions departments; they're likely to judge your application favorably.

—WARNING!—

Do not go telling every coach that his school is your first choice. Dishonesty will only breed bad luck.

EARLY DECISION

Binding Early Decision applications have grown in popularity in recent years. Early Decision candidates apply to only one school during the early fall of their senior year. Acceptance letters are sent out in November or December. **If accepted, Early Decision applicants are *required* to attend**. If denied, they still have time to apply elsewhere.

Not only does Early Decision seem to increase the probability of acceptance, it also guarantees that the applicant will enroll. **To a coach, this means that once a player is accepted through Early Decision, recruiting of that player is complete**. The coach doesn't have to make the argument that his college is superior to the six other schools who accepted the player.

In some circles Early Decision is a controversial topic. Its opponents argue that it puts too much pressure on applicants. Its advocates insist that it simplifies the college selection process for applicants and allows admissions departments to hand-select their students.

Early Decision is a reality whether or not you agree with it philosophically. Its proliferation has not been lost on college coaches, who are always laboring to have their top recruits admitted and signed as quickly as possible. Many coaches now rely heavily on Early Decision to help them handpick their recruiting classes.

Think It Over Carefully

If you've played your self-recruiting hand well and a coach asks you to apply early, **recognize the seriousness of the decision**. Don't let such a request go to your head and make you irrational. Sit down and reason through it.

Thoroughly outline the pros and cons of the school and its soccer program. Discuss the situation at length with your parents and teachers. If you decide that Early Decision is the right choice, by all means, go for it.

If you choose to apply Early Decision, you and your parents should **discuss with the coach what guarantee you have of a place on the team** should you be accepted. Consider requesting something in writing that says that if accepted, you will also be offered a place on the team.

STANDARD DECISION

If you are torn between a few schools, don't feel that you have to apply Early Decision. Go with standard, non-binding applications.

A coach may pressure you to apply early. If you aren't convinced that his school is *exactly* what you want, don't bow to the pressure. A coach's primary concern is to finalize his recruiting class. Your primary concern is to find the school that best fits your needs.

If you prefer to keep your options open, apply under standard, non-binding terms.

22

ACADEMIC ELIGIBILITY

The NCAA carefully evaluates student-athletes' academic eligibility. Approval from the NCAA Clearinghouse is required for all Division I and Division II players.

Prospective DI and DII players don't have to contact the Clearinghouse until the fall of their senior year. As a sophomore or junior, however, you, your parents, and your guidance counselor should sit down and **assess your high school curriculum to make sure that you will satisfy the Clearinghouse's core course requirements**.

The graduation requirements of most high schools usually satisfy the requirements of the Clearinghouse. Discuss this issue with your guidance counselor to be certain.

NCAA CLEARINGHOUSE REQUIREMENTS

The NCAA Clearinghouse bases academic eligibility on your high school coursework, grades, and standardized test scores. The general requirements for Division I are outlined below. Division II requirements are slightly different. Consult official Clearinghouse literature for more specifics.

DIVISION I REQUIREMENTS

1. YOU MUST GRADUATE FROM HIGH SCHOOL:

You must have a *core course* GPA of at least 2.0. Furthermore, to be eligible you must have SAT and ACT scores that correlate with your GPA, based on the NCAA's GPA/Test Score Index.

The GPA/Test Score Index basically says that given your GPA, your test scores must be at a certain level. So if you have a 2.0, you need at least a 1010 SAT to be eligible. By comparison, if you have a 3.5 GPA, all you need is a 400 SAT!

In determining your composite SAT score, the Clearinghouse accepts your best section scores. So if you take the SAT on multiple occasions, THE CLEARINGHOUSE WILL USE YOUR BEST VERBAL SCORE AND YOUR BEST MATH SCORE.

2. YOU MUST COMPLETE 14 CORE COURSES:

ENGLISH	Language/literature	4 years
MATH	Algebra I or higher	2 years
SCIENCE	Natural/physical plus lab if offered	2 years
ADDITIONAL	English, math, or science	1 year
SOCIAL SCIENCE	History, economics, or government	2 years
ADDITIONAL	Any above area or language, religion, or philosophy	3 years

NCAA CLEARINGHOUSE TIMING

Early in your high school career make sure that you will fulfill the core course requirements.

During the fall of your senior year, about the time you begin working on your college applications, you must submit an *Initial Eligibility* form to the NCAA Clearinghouse. Submit the designated documents from the form to your high school, which must send your transcript directly to the Clearinghouse.

After your senior year, submit a *Final Eligibility* form, which proves to the NCAA that you graduated.

The Clearinghouse website has a helpful tool that lists the core courses available at most high schools in the country.

    1.   Go to *www.ncaaclearinghouse.net.*

    2.   Follow the link for "Prospective Student Athletes."

    3.   Then click on the link to "The List of Approved Core Courses."

DIVISION III ELIGIBILITY

NCAA Division III athletes do not have to register with the Clearinghouse. **This does not mean that Division III schools are lenient about academics**.

All NCAA student-athletes, regardless of division, are required to meet a set of academic requirements. The difference with Division III is that the eligibility standards are not universal.

Division III conferences and colleges set their own academic standards. In many cases these standards are actually higher than those of the Clearinghouse. Check with individual schools for more details.

NAIA ELIGIBILITY

The NAIA is separate from the NCAA and has no clearinghouse. Its eligibility requirements, however, are not so different from those of the NCAA. To play in the NAIA you must graduate from high school and meet certain academic standards.

NAIA REQUIREMENTS
MUST MEET 2 OUT OF 3

1. STANDARDIZED TEST MINIMUM:

You must achieve at least an 18 on the ACT or 860 on the SAT. Scores must be achieved on a single test. You can't use your best verbal score from one test and your best math score from another.

2. MINIMUM GPA:

Your overall high school GPA must be at least 2.0.

3. CLASS RANK:

You must rank in the top half of your high school graduating class.

More details regarding NAIA eligibility are available at: www.naia.org/local/collegebound.html

23

HOW TO DECIDE

Admissions letters for standard deadline applications will reach you in mid-spring.

When the time comes to choose between the schools to which you've been accepted, **your first consideration should be academics**. Narrow down the field of candidate schools accordingly.

REEVALUATE THE COLLEGES

Of the schools that accepted you, which cater best to your academic and social needs? Which will be the best for your intellectual and social growth? That, after all, is what college is all about.

Once you've identified the two, three, or four schools which will best suit you academically and socially, reassess their soccer programs. Study the notes you have compiled in your file folders. If you've done a good job taking notes, you will have a lot of information at your fingertips.

CALL COACHES TO REPORT THE GOOD NEWS

CALL EACH COACH AS SOON AS YOU RECEIVE THE RESULTS OF YOUR APPLICATION. Though coaches may have already received word from their admissions departments, some schools prohibit coaches from informing recruits of their application fate.

When you call the coaches, have honest, straightforward discussions. Describe to them in general terms the other offers you have on the table. **ASK EACH COACH FRANKLY IF (AND WHY) HE BELIEVES HIS SCHOOL AND SOCCER PROGRAM ARE YOUR BEST OPTION.**

DETERMINE WHERE YOU NOW STAND ON EACH COACH'S RECRUITING BOARD. If initially you were on the bubble at a particular school, but the top few recruits didn't get in or decided to go elsewhere, you may now find yourself directly in the spotlight. You may have vaulted a few spots higher on the coach's recruiting board.

REEVALUATE THE TEAMS

Think long and hard about the teams you have to choose from. Reassess the coach, players, and quality of play. Peruse the notes you made on your log sheets. Look over the promotional materials coaches sent you—team brochures, newsletters, stat sheets, etc. Skim the letters and e-mails you saved.

Coaching changes can disrupt college athletic careers. In your conversations with a coach, ask him if he intends to stay at the school for the next few years.

 **PARENTS**

Help your son or daughter make a well-reasoned choice once he or she has been accepted into a few schools. Review the schools by revisiting the early literature you consulted.

Look at the college profile books again, do some in-depth surfing on the colleges' websites, and make a list of pros and cons for each college. Which school stands out above the rest? Present your assessment to your child.

CONSIDER THESE QUESTIONS FOR EACH SCHOOL

- Is the **BALANCE** of athletics and academics right for you?

- Do you like the **OVERALL ENVIRONMENT**—academic, social, athletic, geographic, etc?

- Does the school offer the right **ACADEMIC MAJOR** for you?

- Have you had a favorable **IMPRESSION OF THE COACH** throughout the recruiting process?

- Do you have a positive **IMPRESSION OF THE TEAM**?

- When you visited, did you **GET ALONG WITH THE PLAYERS**?

- Has the team offered you an **ATHLETIC SCHOLARSHIP**?

- Has the university offered you **INSTITUTIONAL FINANCIAL AID**?

- How soon will you be able to **CONTRIBUTE ON THE FIELD**?

- Did you like the **FACILITIES**?

THE IMPORTANCE OF A GUARANTEE

As we've said all along, the best outcome of self-recruiting is to be guaranteed a spot on the team long before you arrive on campus. You haven't done yourself much good if somewhere along the way there is a misunderstanding and you arrive on campus only to find that you have to try out, that you're not assured of anything.

Therefore, the significance of a guarantee cannot be overstated. **It ensures that you will be on the team, and that you don't have to try out when you arrive on campus.** This should weigh heavily on your decision. Don't let your situation be ambiguous.

Tryouts are a real gamble. There are countless circumstances that can tilt the odds against you. For starters, a coach might select only one player from a huge candidate pool; tryouts might only last one afternoon; you might sustain a minor injury that prevents you from participating in tryouts and ends your college soccer career before it begins. Any number of things could go wrong.

You want to avoid the numbers game. So get a clear answer from each coach. **Will he guarantee you a spot on his team**?

 WARNING!

Don't try to start a bidding war for your services. The coaching world is small and tight-knit. What you regard as savvy wheeling and dealing may come back to haunt you.

Your efforts to milk a coach for every last dime of scholarship money or a guaranteed starting position—by dangling your offer from another school in front of him—may anger or convince him that you are not the type of person he wants to deal with.

Being on uncomfortable personal terms with the coach is the wrong way to begin your college soccer career.

24

FINALIZING
THE DEAL

When you have chosen the school that offers the best academic, social, and athletic environment for you, **inform the coach that you are going to enroll**. You don't have to jump for joy, but show him that you're excited about your decision.

As for sealing the deal, the procedures for finalizing athletic commitments vary with the school and collegiate division.

NATIONAL LETTER OF INTENT

The *National Letter of Intent* is a program for athletes to commit formally to an NCAA Division I or II college. There's a signing window between February and April. Players are forbidden from signing with DI or DII schools before the signing window opens.

Find out from the coach and the college what is required of you to formally become part of the team. Are you required to sign the National Letter of Intent?

> The National Letter of Intent office can be contacted for answers to questions as well as thorough literature.
>
> (205) 458-3000
>
> *www.national-letter.org*

VERBAL COMMITMENTS

At some point, a coach may request a *verbal commitment*—a spoken agreement that you will attend his school and have a spot on the soccer team.

Top recruits at elite Division I soccer schools may be asked to verbally commit before they have even applied. In such situations, admissions departments will often conduct an *early read* of an application to ensure the coach that the recruit will be accepted.

Top Division III and NAIA recruits also may be asked to verbally commit since those schools do not use the National Letter of Intent.

Don't allow yourself to be pressured into making a verbal commitment. If you are asked for such a commitment, **you don't have to respond immediately**. Take a few days to think it over and talk it through with your parents and counselors.

You should only verbally commit to a school once you are certain that the school is right for you.

Technically, verbal commitments are not legally binding; you haven't actually signed anything. Taking back a verbal commitment, however, is considered an act of very bad faith and will make the aggrieved party quite unhappy.

DIVISION III

There is no NCAA-mandated letter of intent for Division III schools.

Often, arrangements are made simply in good faith. In other words, a Division III coach and recruit will often have an understanding that the recruit will be offered a place on the roster. Some DIII teams and/or athletic departments develop their own letters of intent. For other schools, sending in your deposit is enough to secure your place on the team.

If you've chosen a Division III school, **figure out what needs to be done to finalize the deal**. Discuss the team's signing protocol with the coach.

NAIA

Like the NCAA Division III, the NAIA does not use the National Letter of Intent. The requirements for signing with an NAIA team are decided by the schools themselves.

Similar to would-be Division III players, NAIA recruits should discuss with NAIA coaches the procedure for finalizing a deal.

A GUARANTEE

For schools that don't use the National Letter of Intent, determine what you can obtain from the coach indicating his commitment to you.

Some coaches are willing to draft and sign a document that guarantees you an invitation to pre-season. **AS A RECRUIT, YOU'RE ENTITLED TO SUCH A GUARANTEE.**

Of course, tread lightly. Don't give the coach the impression that you doubt his honesty.

INFORM OTHER COACHES OF YOUR DECISION

Once you've signed the National Letter of Intent or sent in your deposit, as a courtesy, **inform other coaches by e-mail that you have made a commitment to go elsewhere.**

To:	pnzotto@timespace.edu
From:	Samantha Salamanca <sammysalami@newdeli.com>
Date:	May 23, 2004 03:05:08 PST
Subj:	College Decision

Dear Coach Pinnizotto,

I'm sorry to inform you that I've decided to attend Flora & Fauna College. In the end, I determined that FFC's academic and social environment is best for me.

It has truly been a pleasure corresponding with you for the last year and a half. I deeply appreciate the interest that you have shown in me.

I hold Intergalactic Space University and your soccer program in the highest esteem. I wish you and your players the best.

Sincerely,

Samantha Salamanca

LETTER TO YOUR COACH

Take care of serious business first: sign with the team of your choice, send in your deposit, and inform the other coaches of your decision. Once you've done all of this and the dust has settled, sit down and write a thoughtful letter or e-mail to your new coach. Thank him for the personal interest he has taken in you, and voice your excitement about the road ahead.

Ophelia Tawny

1 Gee-Kay-El Street
Baton Rouge, LA 24375

oaf@gkl.com
235|527-6373

Petra Cantus
The Bazaar College
4 Marketplace Rd.
Souk, GA 43671

May 9, 2002

Dear Coach Cantus,

I am thrilled to be joining your team in the fall. TBC has made such a good impression on me. I can't wait to arrive on campus and play with the team.

Corresponding with you over the last year has been a great experience. I really appreciate all the time and energy you have put into recruiting me. All the e-mails and phone calls have provided us with a good foundation; I think you have a pretty good sense of me as a person. Now I really look forward to working with you on the field.

I had a great time with the girls when I visited back in the fall. Please let them know that I am coming and that I can't wait to play with them.

Sincerely,

Ophelia

25

WALK-ON TRYOUTS: THE LAST RESORT

The situation may arise where the coach at the school you've decided to attend won't guarantee you a spot on the team.

You're undeterred—you've decided to attend because you love the school, the students, and especially the Organic Chemistry Department. Still, you have aspirations to play for the soccer team.

This predicament is not ideal, but not hopeless. **Most college teams hold walk-on tryouts, which represent an opportunity for non-recruits to make the team.**

Unfortunately, horror stories abound regarding excellent players who train hard all summer in the hope of walking on. When they arrive at tryouts, they find themselves among a multitude of hopefuls. The 35-player tryout lasts one hour, after which the remorseless coach cuts 34 people.

You want to minimize the probability of this scenario—or at least solidify your chances of being the chosen one.

CORRESPONDENCE IS KEY

Just because a coach doesn't offer you a recruited spot on his team, doesn't mean you can't continue to correspond with him. Au contraire!

Correspondence for walk-ons is absolutely critical. In no uncertain terms, **state to the coach that you're committed to making the team**.

Maintain regular contact with the coach throughout the spring of your senior year and during the summer after you graduate. Be in touch every few weeks to let him know that you're eager to prove your mettle.

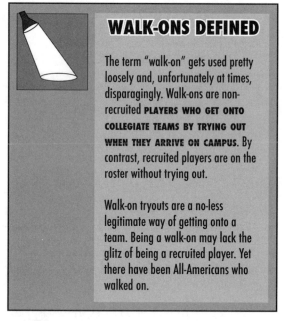

WALK-ONS DEFINED

The term "walk-on" gets used pretty loosely and, unfortunately at times, disparagingly. Walk-ons are non-recruited PLAYERS WHO GET ONTO COLLEGIATE TEAMS BY TRYING OUT WHEN THEY ARRIVE ON CAMPUS. By contrast, recruited players are on the roster without trying out.

Walk-on tryouts are a no-less legitimate way of getting onto a team. Being a walk-on may lack the glitz of being a recruited player. Yet there have been All-Americans who walked on.

Keep him posted on your preparations. Inform him, for example, that you've discovered a regular pick-up game with local college players. In addition to playing four days a week, you're lifting weights on a regular basis, and following the team's summer training program to the letter.

In preparing yourself for tryouts, **equip yourself with as much knowledge of the process as possible**. Find out from the coach exactly how tryouts will be organized, and what kind of timeframe you have in which to prove yourself.

ON-FIELD APPEARANCES

Say it's the summer before you go to college and the coach at the school you've chosen, for whatever reason, still hasn't seen you play. Maybe you started the self-recruiting process during the winter of your senior year.

College coaches are hard on the recruiting beat during the summer. Many coaches travel extensively to camps and tournaments.

Try to attend a summer camp that the coach plans to work. *(See Chapter 16.)* If he likes your play, you will have dramatically improved your chances of walking on. He might even bring you into the fold without a tryout.

If you can't go to a camp where the coach will be, try to arrange for him to see you at a tournament. Ask him what tournaments he plans to attend during the summer. If your team's travel plans are completely different, consider *guest playing* with a team that is going to one of those tournaments.

SUMMER TRAINING

When you arrive on campus as a walk-on, you will have to prove yourself. A strict summer fitness and playing regimen will prepare you mentally and physically.

Some coaches voluntarily distribute summer fitness programs to walk-on candidates. **If you don't get a fitness plan automatically, e-mail the coach and request one**. *(See Chapter 26.)*

ARRIVE FOR TRYOUTS EARLY

Visit the coach in his office a day or two before tryouts. Describe your summer training program and state clearly that you are determined to make the team. Ask if you can observe pre-season practices.

On the day of tryouts, **arrive 20-30 minutes before they start**. It's unfair, but coaches often don't provide a formal or adequate warm-up during walk-on tryouts. Give yourself time to stretch and get some touches on the ball—get comfortable and work the butterflies out of your system. **When tryouts start, breathe deeply and don't worry about little mistakes**.

What if I try to walk-on and don't make the team?

In college there are many alternatives to playing varsity soccer. There are countless non-athletic extracurricular activities and groups. If you want to stay physically active, many campuses have thriving intramural sports scenes. Get a team together with people from your dorm or even those you met during walk-on tryouts.

Another alternative for freshmen is to find a local U19 club team. This is an unusual arrangement, but one in which you can practice a few times a week and remain competitive.

It's rare for a coach to take someone he's cut in the past. If you're committed to trying out the following year, speak with the coach. Ask him what you need to do to earn a spot on the roster.

PART VII

THE FINAL PUSH

Once you've inked a deal with a team and enrolled in the college, blow-up some balloons and celebrate. The real work, however, has just begun.

26

SUMMER PREPARATIONS

After you've been invited to join a team, the best thing you can do is **prepare yourself for the rigors and intensity of college soccer**. At this point you've put a lot of work into self-recruiting. Don't blow your opportunity by being a couch potato.

GET FIT

Almost every serious college soccer team has a summer fitness plan. Most coaches require your participation in their program. During pre-season it doesn't take much to see who didn't do their runs over the summer.

When you commit to a school, make sure the coach has your correct address so he can send you a fitness manual as soon as it's available.

Pre-season is surprisingly short; before you know it the first game is upon you. **Arriving to camp fit is essential**. Even if you were the top recruit, your status will evaporate quickly if you show up in a corpulent state.

Though training itself is outside the scope of this book, the following pointers will help you get through the dog days of summer.

SUMMER FITNESS WORK

GET A PARTNER	It's infinitely easier to motivate yourself to run ladders and such if you have a partner. If possible, work with one of your college teammates-to-be. Otherwise, train with a friend who's going to play elsewhere or a teammate who has another year of high school.
ESTABLISH A ROUTINE	Find a consistent time and place to do your workouts. Expect to meet your partner the same time each day at an appointed location.
FIND GAMES	Sometimes it takes a lot of effort to find regular action during the summer. Arrange to train with a club team or scope out the local pick-up scene. Get yourself regular action so that your skills are honed when you arrive for pre-season.
DO SOLO BALLWORK	College players are more technically advanced than the average high school player. Go out to the park by yourself and get some extra touches.

PAPERWORK

Make sure you understand what forms need to be completed so that you can play as soon as you arrive on campus. This may include academic eligibility forms and a physical evaluation by your doctor.

STANDARD PAPERWORK

HEALTH EXAMS

Each school has its own policy regarding physical examinations. Most schools won't let you to participate in athletics until you have had a physical. If you're required to see your own doctor, schedule an appointment early in the summer. You don't want to be scrambling for an appointment shortly before you are expected on campus.

CLEARINGHOUSE

Once you've graduated, submit the Final Eligibility Form to the NCAA Clearinghouse. This proof of graduation will ensure that you are eligible when you arrive on campus.

CONTINUED CORRESPONDENCE

Continue to correspond with your coach through the spring and summer leading up to your freshman season. Let him know how your preparations are going. E-mail him your times on runs and describe the quality of the games you're playing. Assure him that you will be prepared.

YOUR ARRIVAL ON CAMPUS MARKS THE END
OF YOUR SELF-RECRUITING JOURNEY
AND THE BEGINNING OF A NEW ADVENTURE.

COLLEGE IS A TIME TO GROW AND
DEVELOP AS A PERSON. MAKE THE MOST
OF YOUR EXPERIENCE—IN SOCCER
AND BEYOND.

BEST OF LUCK!

TIMELINES

The self-recruiting timelines on the next few pages are organized around when you begin the process. In addition to the highlights that are listed, **throughout the process you must maintain regular contact with your candidate coaches**.

If you start during your...

SOPHOMORE YEAR

THE EARLY BIRD may get the worm, but puts a lot of time into digging. If you're determined to begin self-recruiting as a sophomore, at least wait until your spring semester before you start in earnest. If you're intent upon starting in the fall, spend that time doing extra-thorough research to determine your candidate schools.

SOPHOMORE	SPRING	Identify candidate schools. Send your cover letter & resume. Follow up on your cover letter & resume.
	SUMMER	Send a fall schedule. Work hard on your game.
JUNIOR	FALL	Keep the coach posted on your season. Send reference letters. Send a video.
	WINTER	Send an updated resume. Send a spring schedule. Determine which summer camps the coach will attend. Register for camp.
	SPRING	Keep the coach posted on your season. Arrange for the coach to see you play in a tournament. Follow up on-field appearances with correspondence.
	SUMMER	Work hard on your game. Go to the college soccer camp. Talk with the coach about your prospects with his team. Discuss scholarships, etc.
SENIOR	FALL	Submit NCAA Clearinghouse Initial Eligibility Form. Keep the coach posted on your season. Visit college campuses. Have decisive conversations. Apply to colleges.
	WINTER	Stay in touch with the coach.
	SPRING	Evaluate the offers on the table. Determine the best overall environment for you. Sign National Letter of Intent (for DI & DII schools.) Send in your deposit.
	SUMMER	Submit NCAA Clearinghouse Final Eligibility Form. Stay in touch with the coach. Work hard on your game. Follow college team's summer fitness program.

If you start during your...

JUNIOR YEAR-LATE FALL

THE BEST TIME TO START—You're probably rather consumed during the fall soccer season. If you have time on a lazy fall Sunday, hit the local bookstore and do some research. When the season ends, gear up for the big self-recruiting push. Include anecdotes and accolades from the recently completed season in your cover letter and resume. Send your schedule of up-coming appearances shortly thereafter.

JUNIOR	FALL	Identify candidate schools. Send your cover letter & resume. Follow up on your cover letter & resume. Send reference letters. Send a video.
	WINTER	Send your spring schedule. Determine which summer camps the coach will attend. Register for camp.
	SPRING	Keep the coach posted on your season. Arrange for the coach to see you play in a tournament. Follow up on-field appearances with correspondence.
	SUMMER	Work hard on your game. Go to the college soccer camp. Talk with the coach about your prospects with his team. Discuss scholarships, etc.
SENIOR	FALL	Submit NCAA Clearinghouse Initial Eligibility Form. Keep the coach posted on your season. Visit college campuses. Have decisive conversations. Apply to colleges.
	WINTER	Stay in touch with the coach.
	SPRING	Evaluate the offers on the table. Determine the best overall environment for you. Sign National Letter of Intent (for DI & DII schools.) Send in your deposit.
	SUMMER	Submit NCAA Clearinghouse Final Eligibility Form. Stay in touch with the coach. Work hard on your game. Follow college team's summer fitness program.

JUNIOR YEAR-SPRING

TIME TO START MOVIN'—It's best to be evaluated by a coach during the spring or summer of your junior year. Get going quickly to make this happen. Include your spring schedule with your cover letter and resume. Follow up within two weeks with a phone call or e-mail and ask which summer camps the coach intends to work. Be forewarned, camps can fill up as early as February.

| JUNIOR | SPRING | Identify candidate schools.
Send your cover letter, resume, and spring schedule.
Follow up on your cover letter & resume.
Send reference letters.
Send a video.
Determine ASAP which camps the coach will attend.
If possible, register for camp.
Keep the coach posted on your season.
Arrange for the coach to see you play in a tournament.
Follow up on-field appearances with correspondence. |
| | SUMMER | Work hard on your game.
Go to the college soccer camp.
Talk with the coach about your prospects with his team.
Discuss scholarships, etc. |

SENIOR	**FALL**	Submit NCAA Clearinghouse Initial Eligibility Form. Keep the coach posted on your season. Visit college campuses. Have decisive conversations. Apply to colleges.
	WINTER	Stay in touch with the coach. Determine if he still needs to see you play. If so, register for a camp.
	SPRING	Evaluate the offers on the table. Determine the best overall environment for you. Sign National Letter of Intent (for DI & DII schools.) Send in your deposit.
	SUMMER	Submit NCAA Clearinghouse Final Eligibility Form. Stay in touch with the coach. Work hard on your game. Go to the college soccer camp. Follow college team's summer fitness program.

If you start during your...

SENIOR YEAR-SUMMER BEFORE & FALL

CRUNCH TIME. As soon as possible, figure out where you're going to apply. Send your fall schedule with your cover letter and resume. Keep the coach updated on developments in your season and your application progress. Try to arrange a tournament appearance during the spring and/or register for a summer college soccer camp.

JUNIOR	**SUMMER**	Identify candidate schools. Send your cover letter, resume, and fall schedule. Follow up on your cover letter & resume. Send reference letters. Send a video. Work hard on your game.
SENIOR	**FALL**	Submit NCAA Clearinghouse Initial Eligibility Form. Keep the coach posted on your season. Arrange for the coach to see you play in a tournament. Follow up on-field appearances with correspondence. Talk with the coach about your prospects with his team. Discuss scholarships, etc. Visit college campus. Apply to colleges.
	WINTER	Stay in touch with the coach. Determine ASAP which camps the coach will attend. Register for one of those camps.
	SPRING	Evaluate the offers on the table. Determine the best overall environment for you. Sign National Letter of Intent (for DI & DII schools.) Send in your deposit.
	SUMMER	Go to the college soccer camp. Submit NCAA Clearinghouse Final Eligibility Form. Stay in touch with the coach. Work hard on your game. Follow college team's summer fitness program.

If you start during your...

SENIOR YEAR-SPRING

PUSHING YOUR LUCK, but by no means hopeless. Send your cover letter, resume, and schedule of appearances as soon as possible. Follow up within a few weeks to ask about the coach's recruiting plans, and what summer camps he intends to work. Discuss walk-on options. Maintain regular contact with the coach up to the day you arrive on campus.

SENIOR

SPRING

Send cover letter, resume, and spring/summer schedule.
Follow up on your cover letter & resume.
Send reference letters.
Send a video.
Keep the coach posted on your season.
Arrange for the coach to see you play in a tournament.
Follow up on-field appearances with correspondence.
Talk with the coach about your prospects with his team.
Discuss scholarships, etc.
Determine ASAP which camps the coach will attend.
Register for one of those camps.
Decide which school you will attend.
Send in your deposit.

SUMMER

Go to the college soccer camp.
Submit NCAA Clearinghouse Final Eligibility Form.
Stay in touch with the coach.
Work hard on your game.
Follow college team's summer fitness program.
Self-recruit vigorously.
Get prepared for walk-on tryouts.

RESOURCES & PUBLICATIONS

A
P
P
E
N
D
I
X

B

NAIA

National Association of Independent Athletics
6120 South Yale, Suite 1450
Tulsa, OK 74136

(918) 494-8828   www.naia.org

Helpful Publication:
"NAIA GUIDE FOR THE COLLEGE-BOUND STUDENT"

NCAA

National Collegiate Athletic Association
P.O. Box 6222
Indianapolis, IN 46206

(317) 917-6222   www.ncaa.org
Hotline: (800) 638-3731

Helpful Publication:
"NCAA GUIDE FOR THE COLLEGE-BOUND STUDENT-ATHLETE"

NCAA CLEARINGHOUSE

NCAA Clearinghouse
P.O. Box 4044
Iowa City, IA 52243

(877) 262-1492   www.ncaaclearinghouse.net

FAFSA

Federal Student Aid Information Center
Free Application for Federal Student Aid

(800) 4-FED-AID   www.fafsa.ed.gov
(800) 433-3243

RECUITING TERMINOLOGY

ACADEMIC ELIGIBILITY Eligibility is based on standards set forth by an athletic association, division, conference, or school. An athlete must meet those requirements to be eligible to compete.

CANDIDATE COACH The soccer coach at a college that you've identified as a potential match.

CANDIDATE SCHOOL A college or university that you deem a good fit academically, socially, and athletically. A school to which you self-recruit.

CORE COURSES High school classes that count towards NCAA Clearinghouse eligibility requirements.

DIVISION I A division of the NCAA that offers national competition, an extended fall season, winter training, and an abbreviated spring schedule. Athletic scholarships are allowed.

DIVISION II A division of the NCAA that offers more regional competition. Athletic scholarships are legal.

DIVISION III A division of the NCAA that features mostly regional competition. There are no athletic scholarships. Team activity during the off-season is strictly limited.

EARLY READ An admissions office's evaluation of a recruit before the player has applied. If the player will be accepted when he applies, the coach can ask him for a verbal commitment.

FINAL ELIGIBILITY FORM NCAA Clearinghouse form that should be submitted after your senior year as proof of graduation. A requirement for DI and DII-bound players.

FULL SCHOLARSHIP A scholarship arrangement in which a college team pays a player's full tuition costs.

FULLY-FUNDED A Division I, Division II, or NAIA team that has the full allowance of scholarships. A fully-funded DI women's team, for example, has twelve full scholarships.

INITIAL ELIGIBILITY FORM NCAA Clearinghouse form that should be completed and submitted to the Clearinghouse during the fall of a player's senior year. A requirement for DI and DII-bound players.

INSTITUTIONAL FINANCIAL AID A financial aid arrangement made through the college financial aid office—as opposed to an athletic scholarship, which is arranged through the team.

NAIA National Association of Independent Athletics. A college athletic association comprised mostly of small schools that play regional competition. Athletic scholarships are allowed.

NATIONAL LETTER OF INTENT Binding contract that a player signs stating his or her commitment to attend and play for a given school. A requirement for DI and DII-bound players.

NCAA	National Collegiate Athletics Association. An organization that governs Division I, Division II, and Division III athletics.
NCAA Clearinghouse	NCAA panel that determines academic eligibility of incoming Division I and Division II athletes.
ODP	Olympic Development Pool. A player who has experience playing for a state, regional, or national team.
Partial Scholarship	A scholarship arrangement in which a college team pays part of a player's tuition. College coaches tend to share scholarship money among their players.
Prospective Student-Athlete	Any high school athlete who aspires to play at the collegiate level.
Recruit	A player whom a coach wants on his team. A recruit who enrolls is offered a position on the team without having to try out.
Recruiting	The process in which college coaches identify, evaluate, and attract potential student-athletes to their teams.
Red-Shirt	A designation for players, often freshmen, who see limited playing time during the season and therefore do not forfeit a year of eligibility. These players can stay in college for an extra year and still play soccer.
Regular Contact	The correspondence requirement of self-recruiting. Monthly contact with a college coach, including e-mails, phone calls, and letters.
Self-Recruiting	The process in which a player takes responsibility upon his or her own shoulders to get recruited. The player takes control of recruiting.
Supported Application	An application of a prospective player that has the endorsement of the soccer coach.
Verbal Commitment	A scenario in which a player and a coach reach a mutual understanding that the player will enroll in that college, as well as play for the team.
Walk-On	A player who must try out at the beginning of the season to win a spot on a college team.

Avi Stopper is the Assistant Men's Soccer Coach at the University of Chicago. He grew up playing soccer on the sun-baked pitches of Albuquerque, NM, and then landed a spot on the team at Wesleyan University. He was captain of the team during his senior year. Beyond his passion for soccer, he studied geology and developed an affinity for plate tectonics, a cappella music, and longboarding. He plans, someday, to be a good guitarist.

There's More Self-Recruiting!

ADDITIONAL SERVICES

Workshops

Hands-on seminars for club and high school teams.

Personal Consulting

Assistance with writing cover letters and resumes, coaching on how to talk with college coaches on the phone, and more.

Fundraising

Learn how you can use "Make the Team" to raise money for your high school or club team.

For more information visit:

www.selfrecruiting.com